T0158155

THE
BLOOD
RUNS
THROUGH
IT

The Blood of Jesus: God's Guarantee For Your Redemption, Provision, Health, Protection, Strength, and Heaven

JAY R. LEACH
PASTOR, AUTHOR AND TEACHER

Order this book online at www.trafford.com
or email orders@trafford.com

Most Trafford titles are also available at major online book retailers.

Unless otherwise indicated, Scripture quotations are from the
New King James 1991 by Thomas Nelson Publishers, Nashville, TN.

Printed in the United States of America.

ISBN: 978-1-4669-0883-3 (sc)
ISBN: 978-1-4669-0885-7 (hc)
ISBN: 978-1-4669-0884-0 (e)

Library of Congress Control Number: 2011963026

Trafford rev. 12/27/2011

 www.trafford.com

North America & International
toll-free: 1 888 232 4444 (USA & Canada)
phone: 250 383 6864 ♦ fax: 812 355 4082

OTHER BOOKS BY JAY R. LEACH

How Should We Then Live?

Behold The Man

Affectionately dedicated to my deceased parents, the Reverend Curtis and Carrie Leach, my solid foundation, who molded my life. This book is also dedicated to all of the Bread of Life family worldwide who faithfully joins Magdalene and me to reach many souls for the kingdom of God.

I wish to express my deepest love and appreciation to my wife, Magdalene, for her love, patience, support and encouragement, and to our dear children, grandchildren, and great grand children. Thanks to our Bread of Life Ministries International Institutes, Churches, alumni, students, partners, friends, pastors and staff, for your prayers and loyal support.

CONTENTS

SECTION I
NOT WITHOUT BLOOD..*1*

CHAPTER ONE	The Creation of Man	3
CHAPTER TWO	The Temptation and fall of Man	16
CHAPTER THREE	The Plan of God in the Old Testament	20
CHAPTER FOUR	Fig Leaf Religion 101	23
CHAPTER FIVE	The Blood Runs through It	30

SECTION II
MY REDEEMER LIVES..*37*

CHAPTER SIX	The Plan of God in the New Testament	39
CHAPTER SEVEN	Out with the Old—In with the New	48
CHAPTER EIGHT	Fig Leaf Religion 201	60

SECTION III
THIS WAY ONLY..*69*

CHAPTER NINE	How Many Ways?	71
CHAPTER TEN	One Way	76
CHAPTER ELEVEN	Carnality is the enemy of the Soul	85
CHAPTER TWELVE	When Trials Come	94
CHAPTER THIRTEEN	Spiritual Warfare	105
CHAPTER FOURTEEN	Resurrections and Judgments	121
CHAPTER FIFTEEN	Rewards and Judgments	125
CHAPTER SIXTEEN	Eternal Dwelling Places	130

INTRODUCTION

In a day when society seems determined to remove the name of Jesus from all areas and aspects of the public square; it is fitting that we hear the words of Jesus once more that He shouted from the cross, **"... They know not what they do."** The Gospels present two questions pertaining to the Lord Jesus Christ which were asked by Jesus Himself and by Pilate of the multitude seeking to crucify Christ. These same two questions are just as important for each of us to answer today:

"What think ye of Christ; whose Son is He?" (Matthew 22:42) KJV
"What shall I do with Jesus which is called Christ?" (Matthew 27:22) KJV

In the plan of God our salvation is dependant upon our response to these two questions. What you believe about Jesus Christ will determine your relationship with Him; which in turn will determine your eternal destiny. The historical facts in the Scriptures declare that Jesus Christ is the eternal Son of God, virgin-born, whose death, burial, and resurrection made Him the perfect sacrifice for sin. As a result of this event, redemption was made available for all humanity. We learn from 1 Corinthians 6:20 and 7:23 that we were bought with a price, *and that price is the Blood of Jesus,* which Peter calls "precious." Do you remember how he said, *"Ye were not redeemed with corruptible things, as silver and gold . . . but with the PRECIOUS BLOOD of Jesus Christ" (1 Peter 1:18-19) KJV.* Apart from who He is and what He has done for us, there is absolutely *no other way* that an individual can be reconciled to Father God, *only* through Jesus' giving His life's blood to save humanity from their sin (see John 14:1, 6; Hebrews 7:25).

Adam and Eve sinned and therefore came under the penalty of death (see Genesis 2:16-17). Thus they needed someone to redeem them from death. However, all those who would be born of Adam, that is from the seed of man and woman would be born in sin and need redemption from sin and death themselves. If man is to be redeemed, then a man must die for man. Since all men were born of Adam's sin, this necessitated God becoming man in order to redeem man back to relationship with Himself. God, the Son, Jesus Christ, the sinless Lamb fit that role perfectly. From Genesis to Revelation, His sinless blood runs through God's entire plan of redemption and reconciliation.

Therefore Jesus, the perfect sinless sacrifice in **His death, burial and resurrection marks the difference** between Christianity and the various world religions through the reality of His resurrection (see Matthew 28:6). Apart from the resurrection, Jesus could be dismissed as a lovable, but unrealistic teacher. He could have been summed up as a person who taught against the evils of the world, but had no power to achieve justice for the down-trodden. But, praise God His resurrection changed that equation! First, it means that **Jesus is alive** and reigning right now, **He is Lord** and one day each of us will bow the knee to Him. Second, it means **those** who follow Him in faith can look forward to **their day of resurrection**, meaning that this life is not all there is!

My purpose in writing this book is to help deny Satan use of his secret weapon, our b*iblical ignorance*, concerning the truths of God's Word. While many beliefs and notions are making their way into the human experience concerning what is required for our reconciliation back to God, be reminded of what Jesus said of Himself, *"I am the way, the truth, and the life. No one comes to the Father except through Me" (John 14:6).* Expounded upon in a later chapter, this is the sixth "I AM" statement of Jesus in the Gospel of John. Here in response to Thomas' inquiry, (v. 4), Jesus declared that He is the way to God because He is the truth of God (1:14) and the life of God (see 1:4; 3:15; 11:25). In this verse, the *exclusiveness* of Jesus as the only approach to the Father is emphatic. *Only one way, not many ways, exists to God.*

Another reason for writing this book is to sound the alarm and help people realize that buying into the error that Jesus is only one of many ways to God only guarantees those persons a place in the lake of fire with the devil and his demons. Christianity is a life not a religion; and that very life is Jesus Christ in us:

- In *Section One*, emphasis is placed on the fact; that because man is a created being, he owes his very existence to his Creator, who in spite of sin remains humanity's only Source of existence. We are totally dependent creatures, created in the image of God with a free-will; which is the ability to choose our destinies. The choices of our first parents, Adam and Eve landed them in a predicament that left a death sentence over the heads of all humanity.

- In *Section Two*, I attempt to show that before the foundation of the world the Father and the Son met in council, the result was a plan in which the Son would come into the world as a man and shed His innocent blood to accomplish the work of redeeming and reconciling humanity. After their sin in the Garden, Adam and Eve hid from God and tried to cover their nakedness or sin with fig leaves. *Here in living color is the introduction of the more than one way to God religions.* In Genesis 3:21, God fleshed out with animals the divine pattern of the only way humankind can return to Him, the shedding of innocent blood. A man must die, there's no other way. In Genesis 3:15, we have the Messianic promise of that Man, our Redeemer, Jesus Christ.

- In *Section Three*, the Scriptures explicitly states that the purpose of creation was for God's pleasure (see Revelation 4:11). God is personal therefore to have fellowship with Him, it is imperative that we know Him through a personal redemptive experience in Christ and His Word. Jesus said emphatically, *"If you abide in Me and My words abide in you, you will ask what you desire, and it shall be done for you" (John 15:7)*. Further He stated, *"He who has seen me has seen the Father" (see John 14:9)*. Jesus satisfied all of the claims of a holy and righteous God against sinners who have broken His law. Christ died for the ungodly! God's eternal plan, His Son's **blood runs through it** from Genesis through Revelation.

Jay R. Leach
Fayetteville, NC
www.breadoflifenc.com

SECTION I

NOT WITHOUT BLOOD

CHAPTER ONE

The Creation of Man

The study of the doctrine of man is called Anthropology. The word comes from two Greek words; "anthropos" meaning "man" and "logos" meaning "word." Considering my study of both Physical and Cultural Anthropology in College I am convinced that a major concern of every civilization is where humanity came from and where it is going. As I grew up, it was unquestionable to even consider any other belief as truth about the beginning of all things than the fact, God created it. That truth was taught and believed even in public schools; while the theory of evolution which holds that human life evolved from lower forms of life was taught and believed to be theory. It was understood to be only theory because there was no true evidence to prove otherwise. To this day it remains theory for the same reason. Yet many chose to believe the opposite is true; that the theory of evolution is the truth and that creation by God is questionable or unproven.

There is also the theory of theistic evolution which holds that higher forms of life evolved from lower forms, but that the lower forms were created by God. The original man was created by God. Man is a divinely created being, God's masterpiece of all creation. So the only true answer concerning the origin of man is the answer God gave in the Bible. God created man and all things; and at death the spirit returns to God who gave it. Your acceptance or rejection of this biblical truth does not change it.

Based on this Nation's worldview of God's creation; when I entered the U.S. Army in 1958 there were only three religions recognized by the Army:

Protestant, Jewish, and Catholic. All three believed in the God of Abraham and each had to deal with Jesus Christ, the Son of God. During that time in America we also had the Judeo-Christian ethic; wherein there was a certain amount of cooperation and respect for the various beliefs even in the secular world affecting all areas of life in many ways. All American service members' headstones were marked with either the Cross or the Star of David emblem.

I recently checked with the Veterans Affairs office and found that military headstones today are marked with more than one hundred different religious emblems. This increase is not necessarily because of additional gods, but human ignorance and confusion caused by various philosophies, and theories taught and accepted as truth, along with sinful perception, selfish input, and choice to reject the only true God. One major reason for this rejection is men and women alike who seek to be autonomous; and won't consider any plan that does not originate in humanity. God has an eternal plan for them rather they believe it or not. However, created individually and accountable to our Creator; each person's belief in this matter will determine his or her eternal destiny. Think about it; one million years from now you will continue to exist either in heaven or hell. The choice is yours!

As stated, the original man (Adam) was the direct result of a creative act of God. Man is a divinely created being, who in spite of the fall remains the crowning glory of the whole of God's creation. The unity of the human race is clearly pointed out in the creative act of God with the original pair; Adam and Eve (see Genesis 3:20; 9:19). The Scriptures state: *"And He made from one blood every nation of men to dwell on all the face of the earth, and has determined their pre-appointed times and the boundaries of their dwellings" (Acts 17:26)*. We all proceed from one blood, both figuratively and literally, for the same blood types are found in all races. Humankind is *one* universal family. Hear the Word of the LORD, *"Have we not all one Father? Has not one God created us?" (Malachi 2:10)*.

All of the nations are of one blood for all were in Adam when he was created. There are only two divisions of humankind: believers and unbelievers. Other differences are only skin deep or culturally brought forth, but all people are relatives (see Genesis 9:5-6). Therefore, no matter what theories man may concoct concerning his origin, God's Word, the Holy Bible holds the only true answer. Man is a created being into whom God breathed the very breath of life and whether we recognize this fact as truth or not each breath we take is by His grace. It is in God that *"we live, and move and have our being" (see Acts 17:23-31)*. We thank you Lord!

Created by God

Because we are created beings, we owe our very existence to God, thus making us totally dependent creatures. The spirit of this world has tried very hard to convince mankind that just the opposite is true. Self-esteem is the most popular and sought after psychology today. Therefore the deception, because humanity is *self-existent* and *self-sustaining* it can live independent of God and others. Other important factors that Satan try to conceal from mankind:

- Man was created in the image of God; that image has been defaced because of the total Fall, but not totally destroyed; and thus human beings have reason, intelligence, imagination, and the ability to express their thoughts in language. Neither man nor woman is an animal! They are far more superior to the animal creation; which are simply creatures of instinct and habit (see Genesis 1:26-28; 2:19-20; Isaiah 1:18; Genesis 11:6).
- Mankind was created to have a personal relationship with God and yet He gave them a free-will, the ability to choose. This fact makes all humankind free morally to choose and therefore responsible for the outcome of their individual choices. From my study of the Scriptures I believe that God created the angelic hosts also with free-will having the power to choose (see 2 Peter 2:4). However, we notice there was no plan of salvation for those angels as was given for humanity. Neither man nor angel was created as a machine or will-less creature. I go into much deeper detail concerning this topic in my book titled, *Behold the Man.* God desired then and He desires today; that we respond to Him willingly by our own volition.
- Neglect or denial of the fact that people are responsible for their actions and behavior has clogged our courts and other social agencies. The belief that man is not responsible has made the criminal appear the victim in many cases. Neither, man or woman can save themselves, but they can respond to the conviction of the Holy Spirit. God appeals to the individual's will, not their feelings (see John 7:17; Hebrews 3:7-8, 15; 4:7; John 1:12-13).
- When Adam and Eve sinned they became self-conscience which gave them a moral sense, to distinguish right from wrong. Conscience means knowledge of self in relation to a known law

of right or wrong. Prior to sin they were God conscience. I believe that because they were created in a state of innocence, purity and holiness, they were ignorant of evil and therefore recognized the truth of their total dependence upon God for the answers to all of their inquiries. However now in a totally fallen state which included intellect and will their conscience switched from God to self consciousness. As their minds began to work independent of God, their thoughts began to accuse and excuse them. Thus, we have the introduction of spiritual warfare.

- The conscience is natural and fallible, but since knowledge has been distorted through sin, it is not a perfect moral barometer. By keeping this truth hidden, Satan's destructive plan is advanced as individuals are moved to deny God and lean to their own distorted understanding (see Proverbs 3:5-6). Self-conciseness is natural and therefore subject to the fall. God-conciseness is spiritual and therefore recognizes that the only true standard for conscience is the Word of God as revealed by the Holy Spirit (see John 8:8; Acts 24:16; Hebrews 9:14; Romans 2:15; 1 Corinthians 8:7; also see my book titled, *How Should We Then Live?*).

- Humans are love beings; who express God's very purpose for the creation of mankind. God is love and love must not only have an object, but that object must be able to reciprocate that love (see 1 John 4:16-18). *We love Him because He first loved us (I John 4:19).*

- God is a triune being, so humanity created in the image and likeness of God, are triune beings. They are triune consisting of spirit, soul and body. Spirit and soul are separate but invisible, and they are housed in a physical body (see 1 Thessalonians 5:23). Upon our death, the Scripture tells us that our spirits return to God who gave them and our bodies return to the dust.

Created in three parts

Each of us is divided into three centers of consciousness, spirit, soul, and body:

Spirit

- Spirit is the God-conscious part of us, capable of knowing and having a right relationship with God. The spirit is the eternal part of each of us that is able to worship God who is Spirit. When Adam and Eve fell, their spirits lost the life and light of God, but praise God; not the love of God. This God-life can only be restored through regeneration, new birth. In this new birth, it is our spirit that is born again; our soul and body must be renewed. In John 3 Nicodemus conversing with Jesus realized that the life signs of Jesus are impossible unless God be with Him (v. 2). In His answer to Nicodemus Jesus said, *"Most assuredly, I say to you, unless one is born again, he cannot see the kingdom of God" (v.3).* Nicodemus's response is probably the same for many church members today, as well as religious leaders like Nicodemus. He had no idea what it meant to be born again.

- Nicodemus was a moral and religious man, one of the chief teachers (rulers) of the Jews, yet he did not understand the truth about the new birth. Spiritual truths cannot be understood by the carnal mind of sinful individuals (see 1 Corinthians 2:10-14). Being religious and moral does not make an individual fit for heaven; he or she must be born again, that means born from above. Nicodemus confused the spiritual and the natural (see v.4). He thought in terms of physical birth, while Christ was talking about a spiritual birth. All of us were born in sin. Our *"first birth"* makes us children of Adam, meaning we are children of disobedience (see Ephesians 2:1-2).

- No amount of pedigree, education, religion, or discipline can change the old nature; we must receive a new nature (see 2 Corinthians 5:17). Those who obtain the *"second birth"* are distinguished from those of the first birth in this manner: Those born once die twice (see Revelation 20:11-15), whereas those who are born twice die once (see John 3:16). Jesus made it very clear to understand, to perceive, or to enter the kingdom of God is impossible without spiritual rebirth. *"That which is born of the flesh is flesh and that which is born of the Spirit is spirit" John 3:6).*

- This brings us to the crux of Christianity and its *exclusiveness.* Christianity is unique in that it includes a life acquired only through rebirth; and unlike religions which are based on the natural abilities of man, John introduces the Holy Spirit's role in regeneration (the new birth). *"It is the Spirit who gives life; the flesh profits nothing. The Words that I speak to you are spirit and they are life" (John 6:63).* The Scripture says, *"God is Spirit and those who worship Him must worship Him in spirit and in truth (John 4:24).*

- We must understand this passage. If we can only worship God in spirit then; we cannot worship Him in soul or body, the natural. In other words neither of these two parts of our being can take the place of our spirit in worship. The seat of our God consciousness is in our spirit. Our spirit is where God resides through the Holy Spirit after the new birth. Upon true repentance and being born again, a new order of life opens to the believer in Jesus Christ; for only He can accomplish this recreation.

- The Holy Spirit begins His work of conviction "moving" in men's hearts (see Genesis 1:2). Salvation always begins with the Lord (see Jonah 2:9); it is by His grace that any sinner is ever saved. The Spirit uses the Word of God to bring light (see Psalms 119:130), for there can be no salvation apart from the Word of God (see John 5:24). The Holy Spirit usually uses a believer to give the word to another person (see 1 Corinthians 4:15), but please remember only the Spirit can impart life.

Soul

- Soul is the self-conscious part of us, capable of knowing one's self. The biblical account of creation tells how God formed man's body out of the dust of the earth, and then breathed into man "the breath of life", or more literally, "the breath of lives" (Genesis 2:7). The soul is the central part of man connecting the spirit and the body together. Until the spirit is "born again" the soul (mind, will, and emotions) bears the major influence upon the spirit and body (through reason and Science). The mind is the major conduit used to sway man for good or evil. Therefore, the mind becomes the battleground between the spirit and the flesh. It is the process of the renewing of our minds (changing our stinking worldly thinking and experiences gained through worldly perspectives prior to the new birth), through the Word of God and the Holy Spirit who transforms us into Christlikeness; which is the eternal will and purpose of God for our lives (see Romans 12:1, 2).

- As a result of the fall, the human spirit is dead and the soul assumes the lead over the individual's body. However, in the rebirth, the spirit is quickened or made alive by the Holy Spirit. If the re-born spirit is well-fed on a daily ration of the Scriptures it will quickly overcome the soul and take back its rightful order of spirit, soul and body; which enables God to rule the total person in character and conduct of life. God's order for change or transformation is from the inside out.

- *Soulish* is what describes us if the three centers of man are out of proper alignment, which is (spirit, soul, and body). At this point our soul which comprises our (mind, will, and emotions) or flesh is in control of our heart instead of our spirit. We live in an individualistic, intellectual, self-willed world which is strongly influenced by the emotions. Unlike spiritual change (transformation) which is from the inside (spirit) out only; soulish change (conformation) is generated by something from the outside. The goal of sanctification is separation from the kingdom of darkness to the kingdom of God. Additionally, the soul is renewed through the Holy Spirit and the Word of God. Continued spiritual growth requires you to develop daily holy habits such as confession before God, prayer, diligent Bible study and meditation of the Word as you live it out in your daily life (see Joshua 1:8). Join a Bible believing, Bible teaching (truth) church so you can grow, grow, and grow.

Body

- Body is the sense or world-conscious part of the individual; capable of knowing and receiving things from the world around it. Therefore it is governed by the five senses; seeing, hearing, smelling, tasting, and feeling. By these five senses people acquire knowledge of the external world, communicate with humanity and care for their physical and mental wellbeing. God's order for a person to find fulfillment is to maintain proper order and alignment of spirit, soul, and body, as subject to the Word of God and the Spirit of God. Any violation or corruption in these areas of the person's being brings chaos. Man was created by God, for God and to be filled with God. Apart from God people find neither their purpose nor fulfillment in life; therefore these individuals become what is so prevalent today in our society; people who are frustrated, emotion-led, self-willed, self-centered, confused and a continual spiritual and physical vacuum. It is God's purpose that the whole person be redeemed. The redemptive power of Jesus' blood will perfect man or woman's spirit, cleanse and purify their mind, will, and emotions, ultimately reclaiming their bodies. Any other way is error!

I know it now

Jesus is not just our Savior; He is the indwelling One who conform us to His image, the firstborn of a family of glorious sons. Being born again, not of corruptible seed, but of incorruptible, by the Word of God, which lives and abides forever (see Hebrews 2:10; 1 Peter 1:22-23).

As born again believers, we are saved in our spirit; therefore my spirit becomes God's territory. Christ has bought me back through the shedding of His incorruptible, sinless blood on Calvary. Not only that, He stripped that old enemy of our souls of power over us. As we yield to Christ in increasing degrees of surrender, and as we abide in Him and His Word abides in us, He brings forth *life* that is not simply *"like"* His own life, but is His very life (see 2 Corinthians 5:17, 21).

The life brought forth in us is a life of faith (2 Corinthians 5:7). Faith comes by hearing (meaning also to obey) the Word of God. A hunger and zeal for the Word comes with the new birth. Just before Jesus went to His death, He remarked, *"the ruler of the world is coming and he has nothing in Me" (John 14:30)*. Having put on the new man who is renewed in knowledge according to the image of Him who created him (see Colossians 3:10), we want Satan to have nothing in us either! The Scripture says, "Therefore, since Christ suffered for us in the flesh, arm yourselves also with the same mind, for He who suffered in the flesh has ceased from sin" (1 Peter 4:1). Your needs are met through knowledge of God (promises) which renews our mind. "For in Him dwells the fullness of the Godhead bodily; and you are complete in Him" (see Colossians 2:9-10). "He who is joined to the Lord is one spirit with Him" (I Corinthians 6:17). Listen, the Scripture says, "You have an anointing from the Holy One and you know all things—we have the power of Christ" (see Ephesians 1:18-19). "But we have the mind of Christ" (1 Corinthians 2:16).

Recently I heard a very prominent TV personality admonish, "Let your emotions lead you." What a sad commentary from our world. As Spirit-led Christians we must counter that error! It's not about emotions. It's about God, a God of action not the God of words that we have made Him! Too much of what we are about is talk and not a manifestation of God's action through us. We are the salt of the earth. There are three things about salt; which incidentally makes absolutely no noise when shaken from the shaker; that should define the children of God:

- Salt preserves!
- Salt flavors or makes palatable!
- Salt is everywhere!

God assigns some of us among the wicked who are in darkness! See, (Daniel 11:32).

Gifts, Talents, and Skills

We are admonished "Walking after the Spirit and you will not fulfill the lust of the flesh" (see Galatians 5:16-17). People are brought into the membership through their talents, kinships, friendships and other ships. While many are coming the right way, through regeneration, many are entering without this crucial experience. Neglect on the part of church leaders in this area allows the children of wrath and disobedience the opportunity to imbed themselves in influential positions of leadership which will eventually weaken and in many cases destroy the church's foundational doctrines. If not corrected could pull the church out of fellowship with its Head, Jesus Christ. As pastors, teachers, and Christian witnesses, we must bring our people to live and realize this truth (2 Corinthians 5:17, 21; Romans 8).

While attending Bible College (after retirement from a 26 ½ years military career), I would often stop by and try to impress my father with all of my gained knowledge. He being a seasoned pastor with more than four decades of pastoral experience would look me straight in the eyes and say, "Son, don't forget the spiritual!" Those words of wisdom stuck with me throughout my own 28 years in the pastorate. When I started out there was a wide selection of people whom I believed met my father's criteria. In actuality I interpreted what he said to mean allowing only those who are born again, sanctified, Holy Spirit-filled, Spirit-led (mature), and properly *skilled* to lead and teach within the church. I can say that it truly is the right way.

When I see a newscast concerning a church leader who refuses to leave even after the people have voted them out, or reverting to weapons, secular courts and other conduct and behavior unbecoming a Christian to settle disputes; I am reminded of my father's wisdom. I believe the carnally-minded people may possess some knowledge of the Bible, but they lack a proper knowing relationship with the Christ of the Bible. Therefore, lacking wisdom, they attempt to solve spiritual circumstances and situations in natural ungodly manners. This is just one example of what I'm talking about. Another is the shortage of qualified people who are faithful, teachable, accountable and skilled. In many churches today the only person held accountable for anything is the pastor and he or she could probably get away if there was not an eleven o'clock service on Sunday.

I do believe that the gifts are from God, but I also believe that skills must be developed. We are all stewards of what God has invested in us. As in every aspect of this Christian life, God chooses to use us and holds us accountable for our stewardship. We are ever learning, growing, and sharpening our tools for our calling. So I have been learning and teaching skills for the gifted and I am still learning and doing. I have come to a growing conviction that skillfully developing our gifts holds much promise (for example, teaching skills). Perhaps there is nothing essentially new to today's giftedness; however new combinations of ideas and new emphasis for this day are being presented by contemporary teachers.

I pray for you who are called [all believers] to the greatest mission on earth, proclaiming the gospel of Jesus Christ to a very needy world. I praise God for allowing the Bread of Life Ministries to take part in equipping saints for their ministry to carry out the Great Commission with great skill (see Matthew 28:18-20; Mark 16:15-18; Acts 1:8). Perhaps you are wondering why skill is imperative. Skill as used here does not refer merely to style and delivery, but also to the collection, choice, and proper arrangement of resources. All who exercises their gifts and talents eminently well will be found, with few exceptions, to have labored and trained much to acquire skill.

As Christians, we come in all varieties. Some have dynamic personalities, and charisma that others do not. Some are more passionate, more caring, and fierier by nature. Some have clearer articulation by nature while others seem to mumble and stutter. Some are naturally dramatic and extroverted loving the spotlight, while others tremble with dread at standing before any crowd. But as Christians, we are all gifted and can develop the skills appropriate to these gifts.

We use the word gift to mean a natural quality or endowment conferred by God Himself, whether spiritual gifts or natural abilities. The New Testament discussion of some twenty-five spiritual gifts to include proclamation as distinct endowments from God given by the Holy Spirit (see 1 Corinthians 12:10, 28-29; Romans 12). Talent means a gift committed to one's trust to use and improve. This use of the word comes from the parable of the talents. So talent has come to mean any natural ability or power.

The idea of skills, however, is different from gifts and talents. A skilled person is one who has acquired ability, usually gained through special experience or a regular program of training. Though we can't change our gifts and talents, we can work on skills that express them. We can develop natural talents and spiritual gifts similarly through training and experience.

We inherit these natural gifts from our forbearers through complex and unique genetic patterns. I have been surprised at times how much I am like my dad. I have made some gesture, stood a certain way, or laughed, and felt the presence of my dad in it. That's how it should be. That package of inherited traits is what I have to work with as I try to become the best preacher, teacher, and Christian witness possible.

Moses complained as one of his many excuses, "Lord, I have never been eloquent . . . I am slow of speech and tongue" (see Exodus 4:10 NIV). But God gave him a pointed answer: "Who has made man's mouth?" "Now therefore go and I will be with your mouth and teach you what you shall say" (Exodus 4:11). Moses was not "born a preacher," but God planned to use him anyway.

Jesus in the parable of the talents acknowledges that we are not all endowed with the same gifts (see Matthew 25:14-30). God in His sovereignty has done as He pleased to give each of us what He chooses. The parable is not how much each receives but what they do with it. Whatever the level of giftedness, each is to account to their Lord for the use of what he or she receives. That is precisely where we find ourselves today as servants of the

Most High God. God has invested in us all we need for the challenge of His calling. Now we are the faithful stewards of His gifts.

The main area that I believe the churches are able to find unity is in the work of the Lord. We should realize that even though we express our faith in a variety of different ways, we are all called to *proclaim the gospel, teach doctrinal truth, and witness by living the application thereof* with one mind and to extend the kingdom of God with one heart. The Bread of Life Fellowship Churches focuses on different expressions of ministry, yet we realize the need to unite with one another and love one another as different members of the same family.

We have humbled ourselves and asked God to help us to prioritize those things that are most important to Him. I believe that the most important thing for the church to do is to *skillfully* preach the gospel throughout the whole world; teach every nation all that He has commanded us to do, and witness to the uttermost beginning in our own Jerusalem.

In His Great Commission the three elements of preaching, teaching, and witnessing become the essential focus for any Christian, church or ministry. Jesus' mission in the world was and is to destroy the work of Satan. His mission becomes our mission as we are in Him and He is in us!

Personal Journal Notes
(Reflection & Response)

1. The most important thing I learned from this chapter was:

2. The area that I need to work on the most is:

3. I can apply this lesson to my life by:

4. Closing statement of Commitment:

CHAPTER TWO

The Temptation and fall of Man

Man was given the place of dominion over the earth, the highest position in creation (see Genesis 1:26). This explains the attack of Satan; as Lucifer, he once held this position and had wanted an even higher position. If Lucifer could not have the place of God in the universe, then he would try to take the place of God in human lives. He succeeded.

The temptation of man

In Genesis 3:1-6 we have God's account of the temptation and fall of man along with the entrance of sin into the human race. The word, "temptation" means "to test", "to try", or "to prove." The test centered around a particular tree which was in the Garden of Eden, the tree of the knowledge of good and evil.

More particularly it involved *obedience* to the one commandment of God. Man was permitted to eat of all the trees of the garden which included the *tree of life.* Only one tree was forbidden, *"But of tree of the knowledge of good and evil you shall not eat, for in the day that you eat of it you shall surely die" (Genesis 2:17).*

Man was confronted with a choice of obedience or disobedience to God's will. He also knew the consequences of his choice would be either life or death. As a freewill creature, he had the power of choice. In Lucifer's case, temptation came from within himself, pride leading to lust, but for man the temptation came from without, lust leading to pride which is just the opposite. It should be remembered that temptation is not sin. It is yielding to temptation that is sin.

God permitted Adam and Eve to be tempted by the serpent, to prove whether they would make the supreme consecration of their freewill to the will of God in loving obedience or stoop to self-will. This temptation was to all parts of their being spirit, soul, and body (see 1 Thessalonians 5:23). The serpent's approach was body, soul, and spirit; notice the reversal of God's order. They now have the sin principle operating in them. Remember, sin was never God's intent; it is an intrusion into human nature. Sin is a spiritual law expressed physically (see 5:19-21; Romans 8:7; Mark 7:21-23; Genesis 6:5; Jeremiah 17:9). Sin as a spiritual law desires to operate in the following manner:

- Temptation to the *body,* the lust of the flesh. The tree was good for food.
- Temptation to the *soul,* the lust of the eyes. The tree was pleasant to the eyes.
- Temptation to the *spirit,* the pride of life. The tree was desired to make one wise, making them as gods, knowing good and evil (see 1 John 2:16).

Satan's initial temptation was aimed at the body when he showed the woman that the tree was good for food. It was an appeal to the desire of the flesh which was a God-given and lawful appetite. This desire could only be satisfied on any other tree but not on the fruit of the tree of the knowledge of good and evil. The temptation therefore was designed to make them covet or lust for the forbidden fruit (see Exodus 20:17; Romans 7:7). The temptation was exploitation or perversion of God-given instinct, a law of man's very being. The serpent kept enticing the woman to break God's one commandment. Thus they exercised their freewill; and chose to disobey God's will, God's law, and God's Word. God's Word is His will and His will is His Word. Adam and Eve fell having been tempted in the three areas mentioned in 1 John 2:15-17. It produced the transmission of original sin or depravity and death to the entire unborn human race. In summary, Satan was the original sinner, responsible for the entrance of sin into the universe. He led an angelic rebellion and eventually caused the fall of all humanity through Adam.

The Long-range results of the fall

The full results of the fall were not seen immediately in Adam and Eve; however, they showed up in the entire human race. Two important factors resulting from Adam's sin should be noticed at this point:

- When Adam sinned, all humanity sinned, for all future births were in him. Therefore, all who are born are sinners. Romans 5:12 clearly explains, *"Therefore, just as through one man sin entered the world and death through sin, and thus sin spread to all men, because all sinned."* The phrase, *because all sinned* does not mean individually, but Paul is saying that one sin of Adam brought death upon us all. In Adam we all sinned (see I Corinthians 15:22). The result is physical and spiritual death for everyone. From Adam we inherited a sin nature; so all are born with a sinful and depraved nature. Therefore, we face a common judgment, all die (see Romans 3:23; 5:12; Galatians 3:22; Isaiah 53:6).
- As sin entered the world by one man; so did the penalty of sin. The penalty of sin is death (see Romans 5:12-21; 6:23; Genesis 2:17). Man was created with a capacity for eternal life and had no reason for death. The tree of life was available to man but as sin was now universal, so death also became universal. God drove Adam and Eve from the Garden, and placed Cherubim and a flaming sword which turned every way to keep man from the tree of life. Even with this judgment we see God's love and grace displayed along with a ray of hope. God kept man away from the tree of life, but He didn't uproot the tree signifying that one day the fruit of the tree of life will be available again and man would once again be welcome in God's presence (see Genesis 3:22-24; Revelation 22:2).•

Personal Journal Notes
(Reflection & Response)

1. The most important thing I learned from this chapter is:

2. The area that I need to work on the most is:

3. I can apply this lesson to my life by:

4. Closing statement of Commitment:

CHAPTER THREE

The Plan of God in the Old Testament

The final act of God in the Genesis account was to provide a covering by *substitution,* the death of an innocent victim, affected only after blood was shed. This is the first place the Bible mentions the killing of animals for human use; God fashioned the animal skins into tunics to cover Adam and Eve's nakedness (see Genesis 3:21).

Just prior to God's final act in the garden concerning man; He showed His love and mercy through a promise in the midst of the chaos:

> *"And I will put enmity*
> *Between you and the woman,*
> *And between your seed and her*
> *Seed;*
> *He shall bruise your head,*
> *And you shall bruise His heel"*
> *Genesis 3:15.*

The term *seed* may be translated *offspring* (see Genesis 15:3) or to descendents (see 15:5, 13 and 18). The term may refer to and individual (see Galatians 3:16). This means among other things, that Eve would live a while longer. Genesis 3:15 sometimes called the "first gospel" because the words of the verse are a promise of the coming One whom we know to be our Lord and Savior Jesus, the Christ.

Enmity between your seed and her Seed

In His judgment, God began with the serpent. While He in no way excuses the woman because she was deceived, but He brought the harsher judgment on the one who deceived her. So the Lord said to the serpent:

> *"Because you have done this,*
> *You are cursed more than all cattle,*
> *And more than every beast of the field;*
> *On your belly you shall go,*
> *And you shall eat dust*
> *All the days of your life"*
> *Genesis 3:14*

Again God showed mercy in that during the course of judgment, He *cursed* the serpent in this verse and He *cursed* the ground in (v. 17). Notice! In God's grace and mercy toward Adam and Eve, though they deserved harsh judgment, they were *not cursed*, God had already blessed them (see Genesis 1:28). The text indicates that the serpent became a creature that slithers on the ground and no doubt *eats dust* (see Genesis 3:14-19). Remember, the Lord assured us; *that we are dust.* Carnality in our nature is *dust* and therefore a source of food for Satan. He feeds on earthly dust! I believe the serpent was an attractive creature prior to the curse. Eve showed no surprise on hearing a strange voice from the serpent. However, this was Satan, the devil, the enemy of our souls; not just any serpent. The battle was on and has continued to rage throughout the millennia. In verse 15 we note: *Bruise His heel* speaks of a serious injury, but in contrast we see that the *bruising of the head* means the defeat of the serpent and his seed. When Jesus went to the cross, He was bruised in His heel. That is, He suffered a terrible but temporary injury (see John 12:31; Colossians 2:15). Oh! Praise God, in His death and resurrection, Jesus defeated His enemy! Notice, Christ's sinless blood runs through it. There is no other way!

PERSONAL JOURNAL NOTES
(REFLECTION & RESPONSE)

1. The most important thing I learned from this chapter was:

2. The area that I need to work on the most is:

3. I can apply this lesson to my life by:

4. Closing statement of Commitment:

CHAPTER FOUR

Fig Leaf Religion 101

In chapter three we saw how the enmity between his seed and her Seed developed in the Garden of Eden. However, we know that the conflict had begun in heaven some time earlier. So when Adam and Eve became the occupants of the garden Satan was already there. I stated in an earlier chapter, Lucifer the angel; who is now (Satan) desired to have the place of God in the universe; that caused him to lose his place in heaven as he was booted out. He failed to take God's place in heaven, so he would try to take the place of God in human lives.

We may freely eat

Satan approached Eve with a pack of half truths and plain lies. The old adage goes, "she fell for it hook, line, and sinker," while Adam went into the deception "with his eyes wide open." I am not being facetious. Here we are two thousand years beyond the Cross and Satan continues the same tactic with the same success. Today, if he can make you think that you can get to heaven any way other than the way that God laid out in the Scriptures, then you have bought into his deception. Notice the parallel to Genesis 2:9; *"And out of the ground the Lord God made every tree grow that is pleasant to the sight and good for food."* These words imply that this was the first time Eve considered *disobeying* God's command. The tree was like the other trees. The speculation among interpreters concerning the conversation between Eve and the serpent has a wide range. Some do not speak of her lying while others emphasize the phrase she added, *"nor shall you touch it"* in 3:3. The real issue was one of *obedience* and *disobedience* to the Word of God. Once she disobeyed God, the whole world changed. Listen to the apostle Paul, who speaks of the sin of Adam rather than the sin of Eve. Adam was the head. Yet by taking a bone from his side to make Eve, God implied equality and mutual respect.

"Therefore just as through one man sin entered the world and death through sin, and thus death spread to all men because all sinned" (Romans 5:12).

The one man is Adam. Through him sin entered the world. Sin brought death. Again, the result is physical and spiritual for everyone. From Adam we inherited a sin nature. Not only that, as a result of our sin in Adam, we face a common judgment, death. The serpent was right they knew good and evil (v.5).

Fig leaf religion

Before the fall, Adam and Eve knew only goodness and they were comfortable in their physical bodies, in their sexuality, in their relationship, and in their work, with absolutely no wrongdoing. However all of that changed when sin came. They discovered *that they were naked.* All of a sudden with no one around but the two of them, they were ashamed (see Genesis 2:25). Their simple, unsophisticated thoughts were replaced by evil thoughts, as they attempted to conceal their newly found nakedness with fig leaf religion. Adam knew the severe consequences, so he and the woman hid themselves among the trees of the garden. I'm sure that guilt of disobedience had set in causing them to be afraid and ashamed to face God. When God found them, He judged them for their actions. Instead of killing them, God displayed stern judgment tempered with love and mercy. We can see the evidence of His love and mercy in the shedding of innocent blood to cover them. *"Also for Adam and Eve the LORD God made tunics of skin and clothed them" (Genesis 3:21).*

Adam and Eve's sin surfaced a dichotomy of thought. This fatal thinking, that there are other ways to face a holy God. Any way other than God's way is fig leaf religion. The establishing of substitutionary death was established by God in the Garden of Eden. I'm sure that Adam passed it down to both of his sons. Yet, just outside the gate of Eden we see both ways demonstrated in the worship of Cain and Abel. The Scriptures says,

"And in the process of time it came to pass that Cain brought and offering of the fruit of the ground to the LORD" (Genesis 4:3). When Cain presented a bloodless offering of the fruit of the ground, we can readily see why it was rejected by God. The fruit that Cain offered came from the ground; which we should remember was cursed by God, making the offering cursed also. Unlike Abel, he did not offer blood to cover his cursed offering.

"Abel also brought of the firstborn of his flock and of their fat. And the LORD respected Abel and his offering. And Cain was very angry, and his countenance fell" (Genesis 4:4-5). Abel remembered the lesson well from his Father, who had learned firsthand from God. To cover Adam and Eve blood had to be shed. We notice the text says that "Abel *also brought.*" I believe Abel brought the same offering that Cain brought as no doubt taught by their father, Adam. However, Abel *also* brought a lamb. God respected and accepted Abel's offering. Why? In Hebrews we learn the answer,

"By faith Abel offered to God a greater sacrifice than Cain, through which he obtained witness that he was righteous, God testifying of his GIFTS; and through it he being dead still speaks" (Hebrews 11:4).

I believe that Abel understood that nothing could be offered to God without a blood covering; just as was required for his parents in Eden. So he moved by faith making his cursed gift from the ground acceptable by the covering blood of the lamb. By Abel's actions, we see him acknowledging that, without the shedding of blood, there is no remission for sin (see Hebrews 9:22). This is why in the first worship service recorded; Abel is called righteous, for in the very beginning of time, we see the centrality of the blood. The blood runs through it!

I believe that Cain the older brother knew all of the crucial truth that blood was required to cover that which is under the curse of sin and death before presentation to God; he was determined to do it his way. Many churches are plagued today by this attitude we see in Cain. As a pastor my heart grieves for the many individuals and churches who know what the Scriptures have to say in this matter concerning our precious salvation, reconciliation and life; yet they fail to diligently teach it, beginning in the home! The parallel false idea of another way through a bloodless offering; which has no life of God in it is a sign of the times among the religious folks. Repentance toward God and faith in the precious sinless blood of Jesus Christ is God's only way for our reconciliation with Him! His life for our life that is what the Father demanded. After it was accomplished, the Father then *looked not on our sin, but on His Son's blood.* Satan is pleased with those who ignore or reject this fundamental truth. The book of Hebrews says of Abel, *"He being dead still speaks" (see Hebrews 11:4),* and he is speaking to us today. His righteousness has taught through the ages what the Lord requires. In these two brothers we see the difference between the claims of fig leaf religion as represented by Cain and those claims motivated by faith in the blood substitute in the example of Abel.

In his bloodless offering, Cain was saying I don't need a redeemer; which undoubtedly is the belief of all who are practicing outside of Christianity today. Cain knew the requirements but refused to do what was right. The Scripture teaches that: *"To him who knows to do good and does not do it, to him it is sin" (see James 4:17).* Listen to Paul, *"because what may be known of God is manifest in them, for God has shown it to them" (Romans 1:19).* "So they are without excuse" (see vv. 20-21). The centrality and significance of the blood is established forever right here in the first recorded worship service in the Bible.

When Cain rejected the blood of the Lamb, the fruit of the tree of the knowledge of good and evil was exposed for all to see. Fig leaf religion or empty headed tares had arrived. Cain was so angry of this rejection that he rose up and killed his brother. Jesus said of Satan, *"He was a murderer from the beginning" (John 8:44).* Thus, we see at some point, Satan was able to recruit Cain into his camp. How was this possible? The Scriptures provide the answer:

> *"Little children, let no one deceive you. He who practices righteousness is righteous, just as He is righteous. He who sins is of the devil, for the devil has sinned from the beginning. For this purpose the Son of God was manifested that He might destroy the works of the devil. Whoever has been born of God does not sin, for His seed remains in him; and he cannot sin because he has been born of God. In this the children of God and the children of the devil are manifest: Whoever does not love his brother. For this is the message that you heard from the beginning, that we should love one another, not as Cain, who was of the wicked one and murdered his brother. And why did he murder him? Because his works were evil and his brother's righteous"*
> *1 John 3:7-12.*

Those who are born again are the children of God and exhibit this truth by producing righteousness. In contrast are those who are not born again and are the "children of the devil," the seed of the serpent. They do not practice righteousness because they cannot, they are not born again. Satan's children have invaded many of our local churches with another way or fig leaf religion, which excludes the need for righteousness. Coexisting with Satan's children in the local church has given rise to the idea that God exists for the pleasure of mankind. We should remember, the church is not of this world; and therefore should not conform to the spirit of this world, and to do so leads to a Christless church. This is evident in the songs which are exclusively about us, our feelings, with intentions to worship, obey, and love, but it is not clear whom they are talking about. The degradation of fatherhood in America has led many people to have more faith in the lottery or Santa Claus than the heavenly Father.

On occasion while counseling young people when the word mother or father came up their behavior and countenance changed markedly, some seemed to cringe at the very thought of mother or father. I notice that kind of behavior is glamorized in television sitcoms and other media daily, that one behavior just touches the tip of the iceberg. Others are so-called venting by kicking a chair or whatever is available be it mom, one of the siblings; or to be fair it might be dad who is kicked. As a pastor I have seen domestic violence in all shapes, sizes, ages, and genders. If these individuals are not willing to hear and heed biblical counseling which includes the plan of salvation for those unsaved, that leaves much prayer but not a lot of talking. People must be taught the truth! The very thought of any other way to God without the blood of Jesus is futile.

Thirty or forty years ago there were certain assumptions made and accepted by the culture concerning Christianity including such basic biblical beliefs as: there is One God who created all things and He is in heaven; He has a Son, our Redeemer and Savior, who died for the sins of the whole world; that there is a real devil and his purpose is to get you into hell or at least for the Christians, ruin your witness. I read in the newspaper the other day about the firing of a prominent pastor of a traditional church because he no longer believed that hell exists. Another prominent pastor changed his view to say that all will be saved when Jesus returns. Why am I picking on the word prominent? The answer is simple they are news-worthy and the more antichrist the better. Satan is pleased!

Jesus covered all bases when He said, *"I am the way, the truth and the life" (John 14:6).* He summed up everything for the counselors or coaches in those words. He is our source; so He is our starting place. We should never assume that people are born again simply because they are church members. Little assumptions like we all serve the same God, and all ways lead to God are error. We serve the same God if He is the God of Abraham, Isaac, and Jacob, who has a Son our, Lord and Savior Jesus Christ. Cooperating with any other god is in violation of the word of God!

If the only life in you is that of your natural birth then you are not a child of God, but sad to say you are Satan's child. The words, *"You must be born again" (John 3:3)* means Jesus gives new life (His life) to those who are His. We can never be inclusive in our beliefs because Christianity is a Person, Jesus Christ. God's eternal purpose is for us to be like His Son. I don't want to oversimplify this but I believe when God looks at all individual human beings, He sees either Satan or Christ; because as individuals our allegiance is in the domain of one or the other, but not both.

Of course you can change domains right now by believing on the Lord Jesus Christ, repent and turn to Him; believe in your heart that He died for your sins, confess it with your mouth (see Romans 10:9-10). It comes down to Christ and life or Satan and death, the choice is yours! Fig Leaf 101 holds to the belief that works, morals, and achievements will get you to God. The Scripture admonishes:

> *"For by grace you have been saved through faith,*
> *and that not of yourselves,*
> *it is the gift of God, not of works,*
> *lest anyone should boast" (Ephesians 2:9).*

Christians have been saved by grace. The grace of God is the source of salvation; faith is the channel, not the cause. Salvation never originates in the efforts of people; it always arises out of the loving-kindness of God. We cannot do anything to earn our salvation. Some suggest that the *gift of God* modifies the word *faith* in this verse. Thus the apostle Paul is saying that even our belief in God does not originate in ourselves. This too is a gift. The chaos caused by this tendency of many to suggest and practice what they consider other ways to God has in no way changed God's eternal plan that without the blood of Jesus, the Christ, there can be no access for sinful humanity to a Holy God.

PERSONAL JOURNAL NOTES (REFLECTION & RESPONSE)

1. The most important thing I learned from this chapter was:

2. The area that I need to work on the most:

3. I can apply this lesson to my life by:

4. Closing statement & Commitment:

CHAPTER FIVE

The Blood Runs through It

In spite of the induced chaos from Satan and man, God has spoken to us through the Scriptures and the Holy Spirit in various and His voice is always the same. It is always the Word of the God of Abraham, Isaac, and Jacob, the only true God, who's Son, shed His blood for our sins. So, from the very beginning as in the first act of worship recorded in the Bible, blood was shed. We learn from Hebrews 11:4 that it was *"by faith"* that Abel offered an acceptable sacrifice to God. His name heads the list of those in the eleventh chapter of Hebrews, called by many, the "Hall of Faith." Abel's faith and God's pleasure in him could not have become a reality without the sacrificial blood. Thus, the divine truth, only through a substitutional death is a life truly consecrated to God. I believe this particular bit of history may have something to do with so many acknowledging their dislike toward the study of history. History is His story! God's story! Satan certainly wants to keep that from us.

Noah's first act

Jesus said, *"And as it was in the days of Noah" (see Luke 17:26-27).* In Genesis 6:5, God saw that the wickedness of man was great in the earth (v. 7) and we will see His remedy for that wickedness. In Luke 17, Jesus was contrasting Noah's day with the apostasy of the last days. How were the days of Noah? Jesus said, the people ate, they drank (not necessarily intoxicating liquids), they married wives, they were given in marriage, until the day Noah entered the Ark. No doubt these were normal or average people, because those things Jesus reported were all normal activities of any society. *"And the flood came and destroyed them all."* The flood came, which was God's judgment for sin.

I see three groups of people represented on earth when Jesus returns, to this world as it was in Noah's day, the *wicked*, the *normal*, and the *righteous*. God has already stated what will happen to the wicked, but what about the larger second group, those *normal*, average, good, hard working, and many religious people who deny Christ, some of them members of local churches?

Truthfully, this second group is actually a part of the wicked group simply because they deny the only way of salvation which is in Jesus Christ. Today this rapidly growing group neither desire God's way of salvation or the things of God. As with Cain, the blood does not matter; they are convinced that their ways to God work. Some are gods unto themselves. One day a young lady remarked to me, "I have job security, a nice home; I'm a good person and I just don't need Him." We must continue to lift up the name of Jesus everywhere, especially in our homes and the public square. Daily more and more good moral people are being deceived with this corrupt mindset of life without the blood of Jesus Christ.

The Scripture says there was one man, Noah, who found grace in the eyes of the Lord. Noah represents the third group. In reality at no time has there been more than two groups (righteous and the wicked). The so-called normal group is really a deception of the devil. Notice they were destroyed right along with the wicked. These people are on the rise today and I might add especially in the local church. They come to the worship service seeking to be entertained and made to feel good, in many cases they find both without the blood!

But God brought a new earth from this awful judgment. Notice however, the earth had to be baptized with blood. The first recorded act of Noah after he left the ark says, *"And Noah built an altar to the LORD, and took of every clean animal and of every clean bird, and offered burnt offerings on the altar" (see Genesis 8:20).* As it was with Abel, so it was with Noah in the new beginning; it was *"not without blood."* Notice, the blood continues to flow even through the chaos. The believer can be encouraged in spite of the continuous chaos of today's world. God is not mocked.

Thy Kingdom come

Sin continued to prevail, as God laid a new foundation for the establishment of His kingdom on earth. By His divine call of Abraham and the miraculous birth of his son Isaac, God formed a people to serve Him. However, this purpose of God was not accomplished without the shedding of blood. God had already entered into covenant with Abraham. His faith being tried stood the test. It was counted to him for righteousness (see Romans 4:9). Yet Abraham had to learn that Isaac, the son of promise belonged wholly to God, but could be truly surrendered to God only through death. Isaac had to die. Abraham had to offer Isaac on the altar (see Genesis 22:1-18). This was not just any command of God; but by the revelation of divine truth, "only *by death* is it possible for a life to be truly consecrated to God."

In the narrative, Abraham left his servants behind with the assurance that he and Isaac would return. Abraham didn't know how but by faith he saw them returning; although it was impossible for Isaac to die and rise again from the dead. As Abraham raised the knife to slay him, the Scriptures tell us that Isaac's life was spared, and a ram was offered in his place (v. 13). Through the blood of a *substitute* his life was spared. Through this great lesson, the flow of blood through substitution is clearly taught by God.

Four hundred years later, Isaac has become the nation of Israel in Egypt. Through her deliverance from Egyptian bondage which was not by covenant with Abraham, nor God's omnipotence, which could have so easily destroyed all of Egypt. However, God commanded Moses to have the children of Israel kill a Passover lamb with out blemish (see Exodus 12:1-21).

"And you shall take a bunch of hyssop, dip it in the blood that is in the basin,
and strike the lintel and the two doorposts
with the blood that is in the basin.
And none of you shall go out of the door of his house until morning.
For the LORD will pass through to strike the Egyptians;
and when He sees the blood on the lintel and on the two doorposts,
the LORD will pass over the door and not allow the destroyer to come
into your houses to strike you"(vv. 22-23).

The people's lives were spared by the sprinkling of the doorposts of the Israelites' houses with the blood of the Paschal lamb, and by the institution of the Passover as a perpetual ordinance with the words, *"When I see the blood, I will pass over you" (Exodus 12:13)*. The people were taught that life can be obtained only by the death of a substitute. Life was possible for them only through the blood of a life given in their place, and this life could be obtained by the sprinkling of that blood.

God reinforced this lesson when the Israelites reached Mt. Sinai. God had to give His law as the foundation of His covenant. That covenant now had to be established, but as it is expressly stated in Hebrews 9:7, *"But into the second part the high priest went alone once a year, not without blood, which he offered for himself and for the people's sins committed in ignorance"(see also Leviticus 16)*.

The sacrificial blood had to be sprinkled, first on the altar; then on the book of the covenant, representing God's side of that covenant; then on the people, with the declaration, *"Behold the blood of the covenant" (Exodus 24:8)*. In that blood, the covenant had its foundation and power. It is by the blood alone that God and man can be brought into covenant *relationship*. What had been foreshadowed outside the gate of Eden with Abel, on Mount Ararat with Noah, on Mt Moriah with Abraham, and in Egypt with Moses was now confirmed at the foot of Mt. Sinai with the nation of Israel. Without blood there could be no access by sinful man to a holy God. There is a significant move closer with each application of the blood:

- On Moriah the life was redeemed by the shedding of blood.
- In Egypt deliverance came through blood sprinkled on the doorposts of houses.
- At Sinai it was sprinkled on the people themselves.

In each case as *the blood runs through it;* the contact is closer and the application more powerful. Immediately after the establishment of the covenant, God commanded, *"Let them make me a sanctuary; that I may dwell among them" (Exodus 25:8)*. Through His grace, they could find Him and serve Him in His house. While God spent two chapters of the Bible on the creation, the tabernacle consumes some forty chapters; and central to its operation is the offering of the blood of a substitute. This blood offering of substitution continued for fifteen hundred years.

Then said he, Lo, I come to do thy will, O God.
He taketh away the first that he may establish the second.
By the which will we are sanctified
through the offering of the body of Christ
[once for all] (Hebrews 10:9-10) KJV. Brackets are mine.
By a new and living way,
which he hath consecrated for us,
through the veil, that is to say his flesh (Hebrews 10:20) KJV.

Jesus, our Lord and Savior, came and removed the middle wall of separation and established a *fellowship* in which both Jews and Gentiles have been reconciled with the Holy One, *in spirit* and *truth* by the blood of Christ; creating *one new man from the two*, Christ's Body (see Ephesians 2:11-18). In his dissertation concerning this one new man, Paul alludes to a wall in the temple that totally separated the Court of the Gentiles from the other areas only accessible to the Jews. He referred to the wall symbolically to point out the fact that Jesus emphatically abolished through the shedding of His precious blood the social, religious, and spiritual separation that had kept the Jews and Gentiles apart. That included ceremonial laws, feasts, and sacrifices which uniquely separated Jews.

Christ does not exclude anyone who comes to Him, and those who are His are not spiritually distinct from one another. The distinction of the "new" refers to something completely different from what it was before. It refers to being different in kind and quality. So, the new man, Christ's Body, includes all those who are one in Jesus Christ, Jews and Gentiles, bond nor free, male and female, are one with each other; and therefore Abraham's seed and heirs according to the promise (Study Galatians 2:28-29; Genesis 15:6; Romans 4:11-18 for a complete understanding concerning the promise).

PERSONAL JOURNAL NOTES (REFLECTION & RESPONSE)

1. The most important thing I learned from this chapter was:

2. The area that I need to work on the most is:

3. I can apply this lesson to my life by:

4. Closing statement of Commitment:

SECTION II

MY REDEEMER LIVES

CHAPTER SIX

The Plan of God in the New Testament

Before the foundation of the world the Father and the Son met in council, the result was a plan of which the Son was to come into the world as a man to accomplish the work of redemption. Therefore, redemption was an action which had been fore planned. From this we conclude that Christ is not coming to the world to be a man in the likeness of Adam, for we know that Adam was created in the image of Christ (see Genesis 1:26-27).

God's double purpose in redemption

The first event in the redemptive plan of God was Christ's birth. In becoming a man, He stepped down from the position of Creator to the place of the created. He is able to die for man and for all things. With Bethlehem there can be Calvary. With the Manger there will be the Cross.

- The redemption brought by Christ is to reconcile all things to God. Since all things were created *in Christ* (Colossians 1:16), God is able to deal with all things when He deals with Christ. In Christ, therefore, all things have been dealt with by God. Though all things have not sinned; they don't need redemption but simply need to be reconciled.
- The redemption of Christ imparts Christ's life to man; that he might be like Him. While Jesus was on earth His divine life was

imprisoned within His physical body and as a result He was greatly restricted. While He was in Samaria He could not be in Jerusalem. However, His death sets His imprisoned life free. Through His death He distributes His life to us.

God's double problems solved in redemption

We have seen how the redemption of Christ realizes God's double purpose. Now we will see how it resolves God's twin problems:

1. *The redemption of Christ resolves the rebellion of Satan:* It is not just the cross of Christ that overcame Satan; it is His *blood.* Satan knew that if he could poison the blood of the first couple, the poison would propagate itself in all who would be born to them. Since the life of the flesh is in the blood (see Leviticus 17:11), this sinful human life has been reproduced throughout the generations. *"He made of one blood every nation of men"* (Acts 17:26).

The sinless blood of Christ contains no poison. It is precious and it is incorruptible. On the cross He bore the sins of many and poured out His blood in death (see Isaiah 53:12). In Christ our blood has also been poured out. Therefore, Satan has no grounds of operation in our lives. The blood of Jesus has destroyed Satan and all who are his.

2. *The redemption of Christ also resolves the problem of man's sin.* Our sins required the death of Christ. His *substitutionary* death dismissed our death sentence before God. His representative death delivers us from the dominion of sin. This is the already won victory of Christ. Though Christ died for all men, the blessing is not automatic. Each individual must receive this gift by faith in Christ's redemption just as if he or she reached out and extended a lamb in their hands to the Lord and the Lamb was the Lord Jesus Christ, *"the Lamb of God, which takes away the sin of the world"* (John 1:29). God leaves us on earth to maintain this victory and to proclaim throughout the whole creation all concerning this victory (see Colossians 1:23).

God looks at the *offerings* we make just as He looked at the offerings of Cain and Abel. The sinner coming to the brazen altar in the tabernacle was *to put his hands upon the head of the animal, thus identifying the offering to be his.* In the type of Christ as the scapegoat (see Leviticus 16:21), they *confessed their sins* over the goat and, in *type,* laid their sins on the goat, and the animal bore them away. This was fulfilled when God, *"laid on Him the iniquity of us all" (Isaiah 53:6).* Praise God, He said the offering *"shall be accepted of him to make atonement for him" (see Leviticus 1:4).*

This offering was an open public profession. Today, too often when people make a public profession of faith in Christ, nothing is mentioned or thought of in connection with a *personal* acknowledgment of Christ as their *sacrifice* or *Savior* from sin. They state glibly that they believe there was a Christ, but often they simply mean they believe there was a person named Jesus Christ, and know absolutely nothing about His atonement. Public profession must be understood to mean that we identify with Christ on the cross and say that He died for our sins, and therefore through His blood sacrifice we are saved.

When we accept Christ today as our *personal Savior,* we do not accept Him only for past sins; He died for *all* our sins, past, present, and future. If we were to trust Him only for past sins and *feel* our works would keep us saved, we would have to be punished for the sins committed after we are saved, *"for the wages of sin is death" (Romans 6:23),* and *nothing else* will satisfy God.

The brazen altar was as; the cross is the place of acceptance. God's acceptance of the sacrifice at the altar is a vivid picture, showing that He would accept the sacrifice of Another in our place. The price was Christ's *blood* on the cross. Will we accept this sacrifice for our sins and by faith offer Him to God as our own Savior? When we do, we are told that we are *"accepted in the beloved" (Ephesians 1:6).* See my book, *Behold the Man* for a fuller treatment of this topic.

None of us dare stand in our own righteousness when God tells us plainly that they are *"as filthy rags" (see Isaiah 64:6).* Remember, it is Christ, not the church; the Savior, not the sacraments; the work of Christ, not the work of His creatures; grace not grit, which will bring us back into fellowship with God. Give Him glory!

Paid in full through the blood

Along with the blessing of redemption, we also receive through the power of His precious blood, reconciliation:

> *Being justified by His grace through the redemption*
> *that is in Christ Jesus; whom God has set forth to be*
> *a propitiation through faith in His*
> *blood." (Romans 3:24-25)*

Notice how often the apostle Paul uses the word "faith." Beginning in v. 23, "For all have sinned [having been born in Adam; therefore we continuously] come short of the glory of God." We can never save ourselves, because we cannot in ourselves meet God's requirements. Our only hope is Jesus Christ. *The bracketed words are mine.* But now being justified [acquitted] by His grace alone; we are declared *righteous* through Christ's work of redemption. Just as we accept by faith the fact that Jesus took our sins in His own body; we must accept His righteousness in us by faith also.

Justification is God's righteousness imputed, meaning put to our account. God set forth Jesus Christ to give His life, a propitiation (full ransom payment for sinners), activated through faith in His *sinless* blood. The word "blood" is avoided today in much of what is preached and taught concerning salvation. The Scripture says, *"He made Him who knew no sin to be sin for us, that we might become the righteousness of God in Him" (2 Corinthians 5:21).* Once we are saved, we will never be the person we were before! Give Him praise!

Jesus can transfer His righteousness to those who believe "in Him." No longer are they children of the devil; but now they are children in Christ. Since the life of the flesh is in the blood (Leviticus 17:14), the believer has to obtain what I call a spiritual blood transfusion in the new birth for eternal life. Thus, salvation is through faith in His sinless blood alone! Again we see the distinct difference between religion (no matter the flavor) and Christianity. Religion reaches up to God by works; while in Christianity God comes down to humanity and by grace provides a way out of their impossible predicament through faith in the work of His Son, Jesus Christ.

Just as in the Old Testament, God met His people when the blood of the sin offering was sprinkled on the altar; so the blood of Christ in His death brings us into fellowship with God. We can now approach His throne of grace in spirit and in truth; brought to us through the sprinkled blood of Jesus Christ. There is no other way!

Reconciled by His life

In chapter five of Romans, we see another blessing of Christ's work of redemption in the term reconciliation. Reconciliation (Gk. Kalallage) Strong's #2643: the Greek word basically means *"change" or "exchange."* In the context of the relationship between people this term implies a change in attitude on the part of both individuals, a change from enmity to fellowship. It is used here to describe the relationship between God and a person. An attitude change on both sides is required. God declares a person who was formerly His enemy and deserving His full wrath; which is upon all men to be righteous before Him. Believers are no longer in hostility with God; because they are reconciled to Him and at peace with Him. Are you at peace with God?

How was God in His holiness able to do this for sinful man? He knew He would give a full display of His wrath against sin when Jesus was delivered up to death, taking the penalty of our sin on Himself. So God raised Jesus back to life. Jesus' resurrection brought us justification and reconciliation before God because His resurrection proves that God accepted Jesus' sinless blood sacrifice for us, and we are saved by His life (see 5:9-10).

Saved by His life

The church has from the beginning confessed that Jesus Christ is the foundation of faith: *"No one can lay any foundation other than the one already laid, which is Jesus Christ" (1 Corinthians 3:11).* Salvation is found in no one else, for there is no other name under heaven given to men by which we must be saved" (Acts 4:12). There is no other source or way to God. This is a dynamic declaration. People often accuse Christians of being intolerant of other faiths. It is so sad that Satan has been able to translate this in the minds of many to a hatred or prejudice toward others; and people are so gullible in falling for such a deceptive trick of Satan. He knows the truth.

The incarnation of God into our humanity to do for us what we cannot do for ourselves has been God's established plan from the foundation of the world. The Scripture says, God was in Christ reconciling the world unto Himself. The angel told the disciples to; *"Go stand in the temple and speak to the people all the word of this life" (Acts 5:20).* "This life" is what makes Christianity more than mere religion, it is a life; therefore unique from all world religions; as they equate to sets of rules or laws. Why did Jesus rise from the grave? Jesus arose to bring us "the life" *resurrection life (see Ephesians 2:1).* Only the dead need life!

> *Therefore, as through one man's offense*
> *judgment came to all men,*
> *resulting in condemnation,*
> *even so through one Man's righteous act*
> *the free gift came to all men*
> *resulting in justification of life"(Romans 5:18).*

That is to say, God's goal or purpose of the gift of eternal life is to conform us to the image of His dear Son (see Romans 8:29). How is this done? God imparts His new nature to us and it requires a process to live it out. The work has begun in us, but it must be continued day by day. The only way you can have this life is because Christ is alive in you. Let Him live His resurrected life of power through you (see Romans 5:10). I cover this topic more fully in my book, *How Should We Then Live.* Jesus explained to His disciples that He was going away, but He would not leave them comfortless. He would send One like Himself. The Holy Spirit, who would not walk with them but would be in them. Jesus made it clear that the Holy Spirit could not come; until He had returned to heaven from whence He came.

In this life in Christ, we have the love of God in our heart and the Holy Spirit is given to us forever. While we are a Spirit-filled supernatural people; we need other Spirit-filled Christians around us to administer grace sometimes to help us in the process of correcting our unhealthy thinking released through our attitudes and actions.

The theology of the early church reflected the God who acts, but today the theology reflects the God who spoke. Another problem we face is the fact that many have turned to the Bible itself rather than the Christ of the Bible. The central message remains the Person and work of Jesus Christ.

The apostle Peter reports, *"Grace and peace be multiplied to you in the knowledge of God and of Jesus our Lord, as His divine power has given to us all things that pertain to life and godliness, through the knowledge of Him who called us to glory and virtue, by which have been given to us exceedingly great and precious promises, that through these you may be partakers of the divine nature, having escaped the corruption that is in the world through lust"* (2 Peter 1:1-4).

The genuine Christian is eternally secure in his or her salvation and will persevere and grow because they have received *everything necessary* to sustain eternal life through Christ's power. This "knowledge" is a strengthening form which implies a larger, more through, and intimate knowledge. The Christian's precious faith is built on *knowing the truth about God.* Jesus said, "I am the truth . . ." The deeper and wider that knowledge of the Lord; the more "grace and peace" are multiplied.

The Conflict with evil

Whatever happened to the prominence given to the powers of evil and the overcoming power of Christ? The church seems to have adopted the world's system of containment of evil (so they think). The New Testament has much to say concerning the debilitating effect the power of evil has on human life, political, economic, social, institutional, and family structures. I will explore this in more depth in a later chapter.

The Gospel of John alone records more than seventy references to the conflict between Jesus and the powers. John focuses on this conflict culminating in the destruction of evil. He reminds us that the powers have "no hold" on Jesus (John 14:30); that the prince of this world stands condemned" (John 16:11). Therefore, "Take heart! Jesus said, "I have overcome the world" (16:33). Greater is He that is in you than he who is in the world!

This conflict expresses itself in every aspect of the human personality and in all institutions of society. As blood-washed Christians, we can be the vessels through whom Christ can address that problem. *Jesus is Lord! (see Acts 2:36).* Emphasis is on the Person of Jesus Christ (notice the metaphors He uses of Himself). The 7 "I AM's" of Jesus:

- *"I AM the Bread of Life"* (John 6:35, 41, 48, 51).
- *"I AM the Light of the world"* (John 8:12).

- *"I AM the Door of the sheep" (John 10:7, 9).*
- *"I AM the Good Shepherd" (John 10:11, 14).*
- *"I AM the Resurrection and the Life" (John 11:25).*
- *"I AM the Way, the Truth, and the Life" (John 14:6).*
- *"I AM the true Vine" (John 15:15).*

Salvation is getting God to come and live inside of you! Christ in you—the hope of glory!

Personal Journal Notes
(Reflection & Responses)

1. The most important thing I learned from this chapter was:

2. The area that I need to work on the most is:

3. I can apply this lesson to my life by:

4. Closing statement of Commitment:

CHAPTER SEVEN

Out with the Old—In with the New

The law was given through Moses,
but grace and truth came
through Jesus Christ (John 1:17).

Our whole relationship to the Lord Jesus Christ must be a new thing. I must believe in His infinite love, which really longs to have communion with me every moment and to keep me in the enjoyment of His fellowship. The apostle John says, "If we walk in the light as He is in the light, we have fellowship with one another. This fellowship is a life that is continually cleansed and forgiven from sin by the sacrificial blood of Jesus. Walking in the light also involves our relationship with our fellowman, which indicates that our walk is lived accountably before both God and man. (see 1 John 1:6-7). In order to understand this new thing; we must review the old.

The Law

Moses led the Israelites into the wilderness to Mount Sinai. Clouds and lightening covered the mountain as God spoke to His people. God called Moses up into the mountain and gave him the Ten Commandments. God also gave Moses additional laws for the Israelites to follow. These Commandments taught the people basic morality. The first four revealed what it took to have a good relationship with God. The next six showed how to have good relationships with other people. Let's see what this looks like in picture:

The Ten Commandments	How to Keep Them
A good relationship with God	
1. Do not put any other gods before me (Exodus 20:3).	Meaning "over or against Me"
2. Do not worship idols (Exodus 20:4-6).	Reject artistic expression and false worship
3. Do not take My name in vain (Exodus 20:7)	Never use God's name in such a way as to bring disrepute to His character or deeds that irreverently misuse His name
4. Keep the Sabbath holy (Exodus 20:8-11)	Set aside a day to rest, to remember, and to devote to the worship of God
A good relationship with fellowman	
5. Honor your father and mother (Exodus 20:12)	Love and respect for your parents
6. Do not murder (Exodus 20:13)	Do nothing with an intent to harm another.
7. Do not commit adultery (Exodus 20:14)	Be faithful in your commitment to your spouse.
8. Do not steal (Exodus 20:15)	Do not wrongfully acquire another's goods or assets
9. Do not testify falsely (Exodus 20:16)	Tell the truth and nothing but the truth
10. Do not covet (Exodus 20:17)	Do not long to have what another has

- God gave these commandments to His own people.
- God did not force the Israelites to accept His laws.
- The agreement God and Israel made at Mount Sinai is called the Law.
- Once given the Law the people knew what they were to do,
- that in their life on earth God would bless them if they obeyed, and that
- God would punish them if they disobeyed.

The Law in no manner changed the Abrahamic covenant, nor the fact that God gives righteousness to those who have faith. In spite of the fact that God's people broke His Law, God remained faithful to His promise to Abraham.

Around 1446 B.C. Moses had given the people God's Ten Commandments, various other laws which included laws for holy living, and the blueprint for a portable House of God. Then the Israelites set out for the land God promised to give to Abraham's descendents. The rebellious hearts of the people (through idolatry, see Exodus 32:1-6) led to forty years of wandering in the desert as they buried the old generation. These forty years correspond with the forty days that the twelve spies spent in Canaan.

Reportedly about two million people began the journey; but only two, Joshua and Caleb, of those who left Egypt reached Canaan, the promised-land. Only after a new generation has replaced the old generation will the Israelites reach the borders of Canaan. This time Joshua sends two spies into the land. Unlike the ten of twelve spies sent 38 years earlier who brought a false report at Kadesh-Barnea (see Deuteronomy 1:19-46; Numbers 13:31-33), these two spies returned with a positive report, *"Truly the Lord has delivered all the land into our hands, for indeed the inhabitants of the country are fainthearted because of us" (see Joshua 2:24).*

These two spies like Joshua and Caleb of the first group were ready to move into the land immediately. The confidence of the spies contrasts sharply with the report given to Moses (see Joshua 2:1-24). I highly suggest you read the entire passage in the Bible. There are numerous indicators present to let us know that God had already worked everything out for the safety and return of the spies ahead of time. Notice in v. 1, the whole in country mission of the spies was accomplished at Rahab's house based on the faith in God of these three people. The three of them exercised faith and took action based on what they *heard*. Faith comes by hearing!

God had the right contact, Rahab, when it was apparent that the spies' presence had been detected by the king. Three people Rahab, and the two spies could have upset the plan of God. However, God uses those people who are committed and available to Him. She was not a child of the promise; however, her faith was built on what she had *heard* about the God of Israel. She moved by faith in her response to the two spies.

Her home was in the right location (on the wall) for the spies to escape after the king had the city's exists blocked. She risked her life by hiding the spies. What can be said of the two spies? They were men of faith like Joshua and Caleb before them. Though they were born on the Canaan side of the Red Sea they *heard* the story over and over about the miraculous deliverance of the children of Israel from Egypt: How God through Moses had them to sprinkle the blood of a lamb mixed with hyssop upon the lintels of their doors. They were commanded to remain inside the house as the destroyer passed over that night, and God would not allow him to touch the first born of that home because of the blood.

While the spies did not have the blood of a lamb to sprinkle on this home, they improvised with the scarlet thread. These spies made a prophetic promise to Rahab giving her the same command given to the children of Israel in reference to remaining in the house, promising the same results when the army of God came through. The rest is history (see Joshua 2:18, 21)!

She gave the spies valuable information about her own beliefs and the general attitude of the people in Jericho about Israel's presence. Her information appears to be exactly what Joshua had sent the spies to find out. The hearts of the people were melting with terror of Joshua and that great army of God poised just across the river. Because of her faith, the *Lamb of God* slain from the foundation of the world met the need for this poor harlot and her family. There is a great lesson and example here for each of us!

- Rahab's statement of personal faith is unequivocally clear. That she referred to Israel's God as *"LORD"* (see Joshua 2:9-10).
- She and Sarah, Abraham's wife, are the only women listed in Hebrews 11; which is commonly called the hall of faith.

All of this reminds us of the New Testament promise *"There hath no temptation taken you but such as is common to man: but God is faithful, who will not suffer you to be tempted above that ye are able; but will with the temptation also make a way to escape that ye may be able to bear it" (1 Corinthians 10:13) KJV*. God will make ways to escape both temptations and trying situations. Sometimes when situations look impossible, we need to stop frantically searching for answers and look to the Lord for whatever solution *He has already determined for us.*

Earlier I spoke of the two domains on the Earth today, the kingdom of God and the domain of Satan and his demons. The Scripture says, *"The kingdom of God is righteousness and peace and joy in the Holy Spirit" (Romans 14:17)*. Think about that, all character qualities of the child of God. The world situation today gives all of God's children a chance to glorify Him in our daily lives. I was talking with a lady a few days ago and though she is a Christian the economy, prices of goods, her budget and things of this world had her really stressed out. I explained to her that it is so sad that we love the Lord but live by the world's standards and solutions; which are in many instances actually activated by Satan's domain, while at the same time the Word of God assures us and promises us that our King welcomes our situations and circumstances and wants to come to our assistance no matter what it is. Many find themselves in stressful situations having lived a life of striving and working out problems and situations in their own strength; but now the time has come to really trust God or go under. Perhaps I am speaking to your situation.

Listen if you are enjoying the righteousness, peace and joy in the Holy Spirit then don't be anxious for nothing. Our King bids us to seek first His kingdom and His righteousness, and He promises all these things shall be added to you. Join a Bible believing and teaching small group and diligently seek more knowledge and a closer walk with the Lord. Your daily prayers and personal time in His Word is imperative for it is through His promises that He sustains us. He gives us peace that passes all understanding. God receives glory from our life of faith as we express peace and joy in our righteous daily living and interfacing with God's world around us (see Matthew 6:25-31).

Faith comes by hearing God's Word (Romans 10:17). Those of us who walk by faith should encourage and be salt and light to those in our areas of influence especially to the unsaved who live in constant fear because of such incidents as the violent storms, worldwide recession, wars, depletion of earth's resources, and numerous other matters. Picture how you would react today if your only source of information was the news media and the opinions of others. The Word of God comforts and reminds nervous Christians how God has promised us His presence and His protection. Perhaps these crises will position the unsaved to listen to the truth and be saved as Rahab did.

There are times when we have to let God work things out for us in his timing. To do nothing but *wait* must have seemed inconvenient for the spies; yet it was certainly the wisest thing to do in light of the danger connected with their trying to quickly cross back over the Jordan.

The Blood of the Lamb

In both instances, in Egypt and in Jericho the blood line was put in place. The families were safe from the destroyer in the house under the blood. God saved Rahab and her family from the destroyer when she threw the scarlet line out of the window. We know the story. The Israelites led by their singers, walked around the walls of Jericho for seven days. On the seventh day, they walked around seven times. They did their part; now it was time for God to do His part.

Never expect God to do His part until you are obedient in doing what you know to do. God sent the necessary shaking to bring the walls of the city down. The army of Israel entered setting fires, killing and destroying, but there was Rahab's house sitting on that little parcel of the wall, still standing! Her house was untouched. She and her family emerged alive and well. Notice if Rahab had not been obedient to the details given her by the spies, she and her family would have perished with the others.

Where is your Token?

It was the token of the blood that saved her and her family; for when God saw the scarlet thread, He passed over the house and *did not allow the destroyer to enter it.* I am convinced that many of our churches, Christians, and families are ineffective because they are trying to do God's job of denying the destroyer through their own strength.

Throughout the Scriptures we have seen that it was through blood the deliverance and preservation came. Isaiah 53 promises that Christ took not only our sins but also our sicknesses and diseases in His body on the tree. It's so amazing that we can trust Him with our sins but not sickness and other circumstances in our lives. But thank the Lord, we read in 1 Corinthians 5:7, that *"Christ our Passover is sacrificed for us."* No longer are we expected to take a lamb for 15 people and offer its blood for our sins and sickness, for Christ took our place and became our Passover Lamb. We now accept His sacrifice and offer His Blood by faith!

The destroyer is identified in Revelation 9:11 as the devil. Do you get it? O How much more powerful is the Blood of Jesus, which Peter calls "precious." He said, "Ye were not redeemed with corruptible things as silver and gold, but with the precious blood of Jesus" KJV (see 1 Peter 1:18-19)? Is the blood of Jesus your token surrounding your family? We have so individualized the grace of God that we forget He began with the family. Is anything to hard for God?

You do your part; recognize His blood and the deliverance He has given us through it. We learn from 1 Corinthians 6:20 and 7:23 that we are bought with a price, and that price is the Blood of Jesus. In this day of despair and fear all around us, it is imperative that those of us who are blood-washed by faith avail ourselves to the power and life of His blood. In this Christ may be glorified through our life living.

As God's children we are powerless and unimpressive to the world no matter how much we talk until we use the weapons that He has provided through the BLOOD and the WORD! These weapons are mighty to the bringing down of strongholds (see II Corinthians 10:4). We read in Revelation 12:11, *"They overcame Satan by the blood of the Lamb and by the word of their testimony."*

If everyone of us who name the name of Jesus would plead His precious blood over our families every day *out loud,* the results would be devastating to Satan's kingdom and the building block of our society which is the family would be restored. This would cause great deliverance and rekindle the fire of God in our churches and nation. Diligently pray and study God's word for therein you will find strength, light and revelation for meeting the conditions for keeping that deliverance!

Fast-Forward to 588 B.C.

So we now fast-forward 858 years to 588 B.C. and the Prophet Jeremiah. Why Jeremiah? We will see the connection soon. For some three and one half decades he has been preaching to Israel, trying to get them to turn back to the Lord. The Babylonian army had Jerusalem surrounded, so that food and other supplies could not be brought in. Now King Zedekiah requests that Jeremiah intercede for him with God.

Knowing the history of the nation; He knew that in the ninth century B.C. a king asked for help from the Prophet Elisha and he got it; the nation was spared. About 150 years later, King Hezekiah went to the Prophet Isaiah for help and got it; once again the nation was spared. Now another 115 years later, Zedekiah weak and fearful of his shoddy band of officials coupled with public opinion turns to the Prophet Jeremiah for help.

God has delivered the nation in the past. Will He deliver us now? Jeremiah responds, *"God Himself will join forces with the Babylonians and will fight against Jerusalem with an outstretched hand and a strong arm."* What Zedekiah should do is surrender to the enemy. Later Jeremiah receives another word from the Lord; Zedekiah will be going into exile. God will not leave the guilty unpunished (see Jeremiah 25:1-14).

Moses had warned God's people of what must happen if they refused to honor and obey God (see Deuteronomy 28:49-68). Now Jeremiah reminds them that again and again the prophets have urged, *"repent now every one of his evil way and his evil doings" (Jeremiah 25:5).* Through Jeremiah, God says, *" . . . This whole land shall be a desolation and an astonishment, and these nations shall serve the king of Babylon seventy years" (Jeremiah 25:9, 11).*

Jeremiah looked at the circumstances and began to pray beginning with an affirmation honoring the Creator, and His attributes. But he ends his prayer it seems as if he is wondering who's in charge here God or Nebuchadnezzar? God answers immediately and His response begin where Jeremiah's prayer ends. God begins with a question and ends with positive statements. *"I am the Lord, the God of all flesh. Is there anything to hard for me?" (32:27).*

So God explains. First He recited the sins of His people in Jeremiah 32:28-35, then He told them what He is going to do. He gave ten "I will's":

- I will gather my people from all countries.
- I will bring them again to this place.
- I will cause them to dwell safely.
- I will be their God.
- I will give them one heart.
- I will make an everlasting covenant with them.
- I will put my fear in their hearts.
- I will rejoice over them.
- I will plant them in this land assuredly.
- I will bring them all the good I have promised them.

Israel was adulterous running after other gods and they were insensitive to the Law. Their witness was the very opposite for which God formed the nation. They had lost their awe for God. So the place to begin in this situation is with God's ability. It's where Jeremiah began his prayer, *"There is nothing too hard for You;"* and where God began His response, *"Is there anything too hard for Me?"* Often with us the question is not "Can He?" but "Will He?"

Jeremiah had recognized the people's problem back in chapter 17. He recorded in v.9 *The heart is deceitful above all things and desperately wicked; who can know it?* The heart is the inner self, which thinks, feels, talks, and acts. It is central to man (see Proverbs 4:23, but it is deceitful and wicked. God said, *"I will give them one heart."* All the other "I will's" revolve around this one.

Jeremiah knew that God was going to have to do something about the heart problem. He recognized that the Old Covenant was an external covenant; which kept repeating "Thou shalt" and "Thou shalt not" (KJV) and man was never able to live up to its standard. Forgiveness and restoration were not enough. God's law would have to be written on their hearts, not just memorized in their heads.

Out with the old and in with the new! Now you understand why we went to Jeremiah. Here God brings forth a new thing (concept). The New Covenant, another way to say it is, the New Testament. Some commentators have called Jeremiah 31:31-34 "the Gospel before the Gospel." The old wineskin, Jeremiah received the revelation for this new wine, the Righteous Branch, who will become our Righteousness. Notice the other elements of this great New Testament:

- His law will be written in our hearts.
- Jeremiah also emphasizes individual responsibility.
- What God does in the future, is dependent upon individual response.
- Their future relationship with God will be based on individual response.
- The future relationship would be based on God's amazing grace.

The Lord says, "I have loved you with an everlasting love; therefore I have drawn you with loving-kindness" (31:3). Here God reveals to the prophet that the love of God is the solution to the heart problem. In His holiness, God hates sin and in His justice, He must punish it. If that's all there is to it; we are all lost! There is *no other way* when we consider God's holiness and justice only, because God cannot violate His character. So adding the omnipotence of God to His holiness and justice will not solve the human predicament. But now add *the love of God* with the *omnipotence of God* and you have the solution.

Sin has to be punished, notice God said His people would be exiled to Babylon for seventy years. However, in His loving-kindness He gave them His ten "I will's." How could He do this? In His omnipotence, He can take the punishment upon Himself; He can become our Righteousness. Praise God, in Jesus Christ that is exactly what happened but not without His sinless blood.

God's love was added to the otherwise *totally* hopeless situation. His holiness was counter-balanced by His love! Love found a way; through another tree, the cross. Christ in our place for the Scripture says, *"For when we were still without strength, in due time Christ died for the ungodly" (see Romans 5:6).*

God's love for His own is unwavering because it is not based on how lovable we are, but on the constancy of His own character. God's supreme act of love came when we were at our most undesirable (see Matthew 5:46). God in His wisdom provided a way to undo the terrible damage done to man at that first tree.

The tree of the knowledge of good and evil in the Garden of Eden has now given way to the cross. And on that tree of humiliation, goodness triumphed over evil. Mercy triumphed over justice. The rescue of man was complete. Man's predicament was resolved, by an amazing miracle. Even though the "wages of sin is death" (see Romans 6:23), God paid a ransom, [your wages] and the ransom was not mere gold or silver. He paid for you with the precious blood of the sinless, spotless Lamb of God, Jesus Christ (see 1 Peter 1:18-19; John 3:16).

He did it all for you! He became your sacrifice for sin. His death substitutes for your death, and then His resurrection to life is your resurrection to *new* life *in Him.* "Christ died for sin, once for all, the righteous for the unrighteous, to bring you to God" (1 Peter 3:18 NIV). You no longer have to live under the law of sin and death; now you can live by the law of faith and life.

This one *revealed secret* brings life, light, and hope to the dying world. I constantly recommend the study of the Old Testament. Failure to do so will not allow you to fully understand the New Testament. It has been said, "The Old Testament is the New Testament concealed and the New Testament is the Old Testament revealed. The loving-kindness of God is central and revealed through out as God dwelt with His erring children. How about you? Is there anything too hard for God in your life? Christ is the answer!

PERSONAL JOURNAL NOTES (REFLECTION & RESPONSES)

1. The most important thing I learned from this chapter was:

2. The area that I need to work on the most is:

3. I can apply this lesson to my life by:

4. Closing statement of Commitment:

CHAPTER EIGHT

Fig Leaf Religion 201

"Having a form of godliness but denying its power" (2 Timothy 3:5).

A form of godliness is an *outward appearance* of reverence for God. Denying its power describes religious activity that is not connected to a living relationship with Jesus Christ. As time progresses, people begin to participate in religion or religious activities; which are stripped empty of the truth of God's Word. The void created from this activity is quickly filled with satanic substitutes. Thus, fig leaf 201 is substituted and through ignorance accepted as the way to God. Much of this deception sits at the door of those of us in church leadership who are called to equip through teaching and leading God's people in truth.

Recently I heard a radio preacher say, "To go to hell in America today, you'll have to step over all of the many sermons preached on radio, television ministries and in all of our churches to get there. Whether that is true or not, much of what is heard today is not the gospel our Lord commanded us to preach. In far too many cases their versions are so slanted by personal motivations and agendas that they duplicate the behavior of the Galatians; that is to preach another gospel. A false gospel (see Galatians 2:6-8) to which Paul thundered, "Who fooled you? Those who engage in such perversion of the gospel are accursed."

Fig Leaf 201

Some preachers would lead you to believe for instance, that since Jesus offered Himself up (the Supreme Sacrifice once for all); as far as they are concerned the blood and the way of the blood are obsolete. A few years ago a major denomination made the news by removing all hymns with mention of the *"blood"* from their denominational hymn books. Therefore, by excluding the blood of Jesus they are suggesting the possibility of another way to be saved. I call this thinking "Fig Leaf Religion 201" because it's the same old "Fig Leaf Religion 101" found in the Old Testament just advanced and repackaged by Satan for New Testament times, the last days.

Notice how Jesus exposes Satan's deception. Then Jesus said unto those Jews who believed Him, *"If you abide in My word, you are My disciples indeed. And you shall know the truth, and the truth shall make you free." They answered Him, "We are Abraham's descendents, and have never been in bondage to anyone. How can you say, "You will be free?"(see John 8:31-33).*

Satan plays his game of deception right up to the end; and as he did then he continues today fooling religious folks; who believe they are free by pedigree, and accepted by God, apart from the *blood of Jesus Christ.* For those in Christ he strives to arrest their spiritual development through discouragement, bullying or any trick that works for him. Jesus further reveals Satan's hidden deception in verse 44, saying,

> *"You are of your father the devil,*
> *and the desires of your father you want to do.*
> *He was a murderer from the beginning,*
> *and does not stand in the truth,*
> *because there is no truth in him.*
> *When he speaks a lie,*
> *he speaks from his own resources,*
> *for he is a liar and the father of it."*

The claims of these people to be descendents of Abraham were futile, because their deeds and lifestyles evidenced the absence of any moral relationship to Him. If they were truly children of God, surely they would have reverenced the Son of God. Yet, their reaction against Jesus only revealed the truth that the devil was their father. As I stated above, it is neither ethnic nor family pedigree that makes one acceptable to God, but honoring God by loving and believing in His Son.

Notice how the enemy tried to put pressure on Jesus about His own legitimacy. He uses these same suggestive tactics today forcing people to cooperate with his worldly agendas and systems; though they are often unaware of what is actually taking place. There are many people in the churches who allow him to bluff them over past sins or as in this case, some so-called illegitimacy.

Among Satan's major deceptions today, we hear such suggestive ways for the autonomous "self" to reach God and heaven through:

- Moral behavior
- Benevolence
- Church attendance
- Works
- Biblical knowledge (alone)
- Keeping the Ten Commandments
- Experience and reason

Notice these are all fruits of the tree of the knowledge of good and evil. All are natural attempts or (forms of godliness). While they are good and commendable for the purpose in which they were designed to function; Adam's fig leaves are proof enough that they are insufficient and without hope. Though Satan knows this, he probably thinks it will still work due to humankind's ignorance of God's truth. He knows that our only *hope* is Jesus, the only Way to God.

Jesus, the only Way

The moment a person trusts in Christ, that person receives the Holy Spirit (see Romans 8:9), who constantly encourages him or her in their *hope* in God. If God so loved us when we were without strength, helpless, ungodly enemies of His, how much more will He love us once we are His children? *By His blood . . . through the death of His Son (see Romans 5:10)* we have been justified. So as I stated earlier, we are declared righteous and reconciled, meaning our state of alienation from God has been changed. Believers are no longer enemies of God; they are at *peace with God (see v.1).*

The second part of verse 10 says, *we will be saved by His life.* To experience this truth, the believer must fully cooperate with the process that is explained in Romans 6:1-14). In that Scripture, the believer's identification with Christ means being identified with His death, then it follows that the believer also identifies with Jesus' resurrection.

Having died to sin and having been raised with Christ, the believer who was once enslaved to the power of sin is now by God's grace placed in Christ and the Holy Spirit is placed in the believer. We are quickened or made alive by the Holy Spirit. So the conclusion of the matter is:

- It is by the blood of Jesus that we died.
- It is by the blood of Jesus that we live.

Dying and living with Christ introduces a new idea. Therefore, Christians must not only know that they have died to sin (vv. 3-7) and have been made alive with Christ, they must also *believe it.* We must agree with the apostle Paul, "not I but Christ." I've died to self and now it is He who lives within me. His purpose now becomes my purpose. New life in Christ is the only way to God! This new life points to two aspects of Jesus.

Two Aspects of Jesus

In 2 Corinthians 5:16, Paul tells us, *"Therefore, from now on, we regard no one according to the flesh. Even though we have known Christ according to the flesh, yet now we know Him thus no longer."* "According to the flesh" suggests external evaluation viewed from an earthly perspective. The *first aspect,* fig leaf religion loves the Jesus of Galilee as seen in the natural, who healed the sick, gave sight to the blind, fed the 5000, and proved by association that He loved all humanity. The last view the world had of Him was on Calvary crucified as a criminal. So many I'm sure remembered Him as a good man, great teacher and social activist. However, that's as far as their natural love can carry them.

The church is reeling today because of this religion; which only requires respectability to the self. They base their theology on Jesus' love for the poor as evidenced by His social action. People flock to ministries and churches that foster this theology. There is no moral accountability required; rather it is strictly based on humanitarian works. This was the situation at

Corinth. Believers were judging after the flesh (see 1 Corinthians 4:1-7). They were comparing Paul with other teachers and using carnal judgment instead of spiritual discernment. As so many in the church do today, they were forgetting that the Christian life is a *new creation* with new values and motives (see 2 Corinthians 5:17).

The *second aspect* is what it means to be a Christian. Christ's *death* and *resurrection* for us, and our identification with Him by faith makes existence as a new creation possible. Our relationship with Christ in the new birth affects every aspect of life. Paul, as an unconverted Jewish rabbi, probably did look upon Christ after the flesh. But after his Damascus road experience, seeing the glorified Christ changed Paul's point of view. Certainly, as Christians this should speak to our perspective of Christ. We must have a spiritual evaluation based on the Word of God and our personal relationship with Christ. Blood-washed, Spirit-filled, Christ-like Christians are the ultimate goal.

This chapter reveals numerous motives that controlled Paul's life and ministry. He was so overwhelmed by Jesus' love for him that to serve and honor Christ became the chief controlling motive of his life. We would do well to apply them to our lives as well:

- Christ's love for us
- Our love for Christ
- Our confidence of heaven
- Our concern to please Christ

There can be no selfishness in the heart of the Christian who understands the love of Christ. Lest we forget why Jesus died:

- That we might live *through* Him (see 1 John 4:9).
- That we might live *with* Him (see 1 Thessalonians 5:10).
- That we might live *for* Him (see 2 Corinthians 5:15).

Christ stated that His ultimate purpose in coming to earth is to destroy the works of Satan. At His ultimate purpose the world hates Jesus. Paul knew that to follow Jesus in our own strength and try to fulfill His purpose was and is impossible. Therefore, he admonishes us to *"Walk in the Spirit, and you shall not fulfill the lust of the flesh"* (Romans 5:16).

The only consistent way to overcome, and be useful to Christ's purpose is to live step-by-step in the power of the Holy Spirit as He works through our spirit. Walking each moment by faith in God's Word under the Holy Spirit's control assures absolute victory over the sinful nature; which is diametrically opposed to God's plan and purpose. Those who have mastered this are those who keep their focus on the Lord.

In Colossians 1:9-13, Paul further tells us to walk worthy of the Lord this requires:

- That you be filled with the knowledge of His will in all wisdom and spiritual understanding (also see 2 Peter 1:3).
- A radical commitment of our will and disposition to please Christ (also see John 8:29).
- Fruitful in every good work and increasing in the knowledge of God (also see Galatians 5:23).
- Strengthened with all might, according to His glorious power.
- Giving thanks to the Father who has *qualified* us to be partakers of the inheritance of the saints in the light.

The word *qualified* means to be able or authorized for a task. Believers can *never* be qualified on their own; but it is God who qualifies us through His Son. Oh! How Satan would love to hide that truth. Please note the tense of this word denotes and act or event in the past rather than a process. Here we can see why Christianity must be exclusive! It is imperative on our part as church leaders not to allow any secular thought, hypocrisies, nor demonically influenced deceptions to move the church from the truth of God's Word and kingdom mandate.

We are to remember Jesus' discourse of the seeds in Matthew 13:38-43, there He explained that the seeds are sown into the field which is the world, not the church! The church is in the world but not of the world. Therefore, our direction comes from the Word of God and not the world's secular thought. Certainly some tares are in the local churches, but they should not be allowed to function in any spiritual or authoritative positions. First of all remember who their daddy is! It behooves us to be ever thankful that we are made partakers of the inheritance of the saints (see v.12).

In verse 13, God has conveyed the truth that He has liberated the believers from under Satan's authority to Christ's authority, describing a movement from the kingdom of darkness into the kingdom of the Son of His love. So the *true* church is in the kingdom of Christ. Ensuing verses describe what Christ's redemption has accomplished in those who are

His, bringing us to a place of "completeness" of spiritual adequacy, and authority. He also gives us the ability to live victoriously over and above the invisible powers of the kingdom of darkness (see vv. 14-16; 2:6-10). We are freed from bondage to sin by forgiveness of sins through the *blood* of Jesus Christ (see Ephesians 1:7).

Firstborn over all Creation

The words in Colossians 1:15-17 which form an early church hymn of praise do not describe Christ as the first being created in time because it proclaims that all things were "created by Him" and that "He is before all things." Following the celebration of Christ's superiority over all creation, the hymn moves on to proclaim His authority over the church. He is the *head* of His own *body,* which is the church. Not only did Jesus create all things; but everything was created for His purposes. He is said to be the "heir of all things" (see Hebrews 1:2).

Listen to the counsel of Hebrews 12:1-2, *Therefore we also, since we are surrounded by so great a cloud of witnesses, "let us lay aside every weight, and the sin which so easily ensnares us, and let us run with endurance the race that is set before us, looking unto Jesus, the author and finisher of our faith, who for the joy that was set before Him endured the cross, despising the shame, and has sat down at the right hand of the throne of God."*

In other words, get your eyes off yourself—both your sins and good works—and don't let anything distract you from Christ. The cloud of witnesses refers to the men and women of faith mentioned in Hebrews 11:2, who are witnesses testifying to the truth of the faith. Weight is anything that hinders our forward and upward progress. Looking means *"fixing our eyes trustingly"* upon Christ rather than our circumstances. He began this work in us, let Him finish it! You cannot be a Christian without believing that Jesus Christ is God. He Himself said,

> *"I said therefore, unto you, that ye shall die in*
> *your sins; for if ye believe not that I am He,*
> *ye shall die in your sins (John 8:24) KJV.*

Personal Journal Notes (Reflection & Responses)

1. The most important thing I learned from this chapter was:

2. The area that I need to work on the most is:

3. I can apply this lesson to my life by:

4. Closing statement of Commitment:

SECTION III

THIS WAY ONLY

CHAPTER NINE

How Many Ways?

"You shall have no other gods before Me" (Exodus 20:3)

God claims an exclusive right to be acknowledged as the only God to be worshipped. Meaning we are to have no other god(s) in addition to Him. If we are to enjoy a properly ordered life, this relationship of His preeminence is the foundation.

Both the Old and the New Testaments begin with the devil tempting someone to break this commandment of God. In Genesis, Satan tells Eve that she will become like God if she eat of the fruit of the tree of the knowledge of good and evil (see Genesis 3:1-6).

In the Gospel of Matthew, as Jesus prepared to embark upon His public ministry, the devil tempted Him to substitute His trust in the plan of God, for worship and trust in his provision. Jesus abruptly refused this temptation (see Matthew 4:8-11). Here two millennia later, though he is a defeated foe, Satan, the enemy of our souls continues to tempt us into filling our lives with everything but God.

The Scripture explicitly states that the purpose of creation was for God's pleasure (see Revelation 4:11). Therefore to have fellowship with Him, it is imperative that we know Him. *Philip said to Him, "Lord, show us the Father, and it is sufficient for us." Jesus said unto him, "Have I been with you so long; and yet you have not known Me, Philip? "He who has seen me has seen the Father" (see John 14:9).*

The God of the New Testament

God has revealed that He exists as one God in three eternal and equal persons in the Godhead. Christianity calls this the Holy Trinity: God the Father, God the Son, and God the Holy Spirit. While the word *trinity* is not found in the Bible, its truth is well established. Notice:

- Each Person of the Godhead is called God (see 1 Corinthians 8:6; Hebrews 1:8; Acts 5:3-4).
- Each Person of the Godhead has the same divine attributes (see Romans 16:26; John 8:58; Hebrews 9:14).
- Each Person of the Godhead is involved in the same divine work in believers (see Romans 8:26-27).
- Each Person of the Godhead was involved in the creation (see John 1:1-4).

The New Testament brings full revelation in the person of Jesus Christ all that was typified in the Old Testament's fifteen hundred year mediatory ministry. The word "mediator" is used several times in the epistles, each time referring to the Son of God. A mediator is a "middle man" or one that interposes between parties who are in conflict, for the purpose of reconciling them. Thus Jesus is the Go-between or Mediator between God and man.

- "For there is one God and one Mediator between God and man, the Man Jesus Christ" (see 1 Timothy 2:5).
- "Jesus Christ is "the Mediator of the New Testament" (see Hebrews 9:15; 8:6).
- The author of Hebrews declares that we are come "to Jesus the Mediator of the New Covenant" (see Hebrews 12:24; Galatians 3:19-20).

Jesus Christ, the Divine-Human Mediator

Christ was a sinless Mediator in contrast to Moses and Aaron, both of whom needed redemption for sins themselves. He was a perfect Mediator as a divine-human person. It is imperative that a mediator understand the total circumstances and positions of both parties in the conflict. He must be able to identify fully with both in order to effectively mediate between them. I cover this in much more detail in my book *"Behold The Man."*

Jesus Christ was the God-man. He was God, having the nature of God and therefore identifying with God and His absolute holiness. He also became man, thus identifying with man in His sinless humanity. This divine-human nature qualifies Him to be the perfect mediator between God and man.

> *"Therefore in all things He had*
> *to be made like His brethren,*
> *that He might be a merciful and faithful*
> *High Priest in things pertaining to God,*
> *to make propitiation*
> *for the sins of the people.*
> *For in that He Himself has suffered, being tempted,*
> *He is able to aid those who are tempted"*
> *(Hebrews 2:17-18).*

Make propitiation in this passage refers to the satisfaction of the claims of a holy and righteous God against sinners who have broken His law. Christ appeased God's righteous wrath by shedding His blood on the cross in our place (see Romans 3:21-26). Although He was completely perfect and sinless; Christ voluntarily submitted to His agonizing *death,* the penalty for sin. This voluntary *sacrifice* of Himself for our welfare satisfied the justice and holiness of God.

Christ's suffering included temptation. He experienced the lure of sin, but He never surrendered Himself to it. He knows what it is to be tempted, so He knows how to help those who are tempted.

Right here, the atonement or work of Christ, is where many churches meet their spiritual Waterloo. People have the moral and spiritual freedom to live on either the positive or negative side of any biblical truth. However, it is not the privilege of any Christian to adopt that attitude. Yet, in the atonement we readily see that many choose the negative side; which blinds them to truth. A saying that rang throughout the halls of my alma mater was, *"God's methods change but His principles [truths] remain the same."*

There is a satanic deception that is very subtly making its way through some churches. It denies the necessity of the atonement of Christ as a prerequisite for entry into the kingdom of God. Satan knows that without the atonement the local church is a mere social club; where the only alternative to true worship and the Gospel, is bringing worship down to simply telling them what they want to hear, providing entertainment, and making them feel good.

Denying those foundational truths by thinking; they will go away or time will take care of them is futile (see Romans 1:20-23). It has been said that Christianity is only one generation away from extinction. That is to say; if just one generation of a family, a church, or a culture fails to share or pass on the Gospel to the next generation, then extinction happens. Certainly if not extinct, it will be so distorted that the people will not know what to believe. This nation is moving at a very fast pace toward reaching that state. Please notice once the blood is taken out the whole thing collapses. In God's plan the blood is always central, present and runs through it (see Hebrews 9:16-22). All church leadership must remember; it is the responsibility of the Christian church to hold to the foundational principles of the Christian faith, and to communicate these unchanging truths to the present generation.

PERSONAL JOURNAL NOTES (REFLECTION & RESPONSE)

1. The most important thing I learned from this chapter was:

2. The area that I need to work on the most is:

3. I can apply this lesson to my life by:

4. Closing statement of Commitment:

CHAPTER TEN

One Way

Two thousand years ago, the Apostle Paul said, *"For the Jews require a sign and the Greeks seek after wisdom"* *(1 Corinthians 1:22)*. This is true today. If we are going to impact this generation with the Gospel, then our message must be accompanied by "a demonstration of the Spirit's power; so faith does not rest solely on human wisdom but God's power. Paul informs,

> *"And my speech and my preaching was not with enticing words*
> *of man's wisdom,*
> *but in demonstration of the Spirit and of power.*
> *That your faith should not stand in the wisdom of man,*
> *but in the power of God" (1 Corinthians 2:4-5).*

Operating in the power of God

If we are going to impact this generation of young people with the Gospel of Jesus Christ, then our message must be fitted to operate not only in the fellowship of His suffering, but also in the power of His resurrection. That is to say,

- Not in the wisdom of men

- But in the power of God

Most Christians are experiencing Jesus as the Lamb of God, not as the Lion of Judah. This equates to fellowship without the power of His resurrection, in other words, we are left with the same picture of the Savior that the world last saw of Him (Christ dead on the cross). We are reminded by the Scriptures, when we commune together the bread represents His broken body, while the cup symbolizes His blood. We are told to remember what Christ accomplished on the cross through His shed blood. If we are not careful we'll find ourselves "settling for a form of godliness that lacks power."

While we are remembering, let us not forget His resurrection with power; and because we were in Him as He died and was buried; so we were also in Him in Hs resurrection. Christ is alive forever more! He is our Lord and Savior. He stated emphatically that *"whosoever believes in me will do the works I have been doing, and they will do even greater things than these"* (John 14:12).

Power-packed faith

These greater things included operating in the supernatural power of God; through healing, signs, and wonders for the purpose of drawing people to Jesus and demonstrating the grace and goodness of God and His kingdom (see Matthew 10:1). It is not enough to teach our young people of the Lord's presence and power; we must also allow them to see them demonstrated through our lives. The wisdom of men only yields a powerless, anemic faith. These young Christians are seeking more and they should get it! How? Let me offer three Keys that will enable them to operate in the supernatural and resurrection power of God, knowing by revelation that they are not struggling to get up to heaven; rather, to be positioned correctly in their relationship with the Almighty (see Ephesians 2:6). You were born in heaven in spiritual rebirth (see John 3:1-8). To be effective in your walk in fulfilling the kingdom mandate you must recognize that it is not you that the devil is afraid of, it is Christ in you! This must be imbedded in the hearts of all Christians if we are to represent Him well in this world.

1. The first key is to understand the delegated power and authority
    that Jesus promised those who believe in Him:

    - *The Holy Spirit:* The apostles' mission of spreading the gospel
      was the major reason the Holy Spirit empowered them.
      While they had already experienced the Holy Spirit's saving,
      guiding, teaching, and miracle-working power. Soon they
      would receive His indwelling presence and a new dimension
      of power for *witness* (see Acts 1:8; John 16:7-15).
    - *The name of Jesus:* The Scriptures attest to certain *signs* that
      follow the gospel message and confirm to the people that
      the ministries of Christ's ambassadors are truthful in every
      generation. Magdalene and I worked with the Reverend Tom
      and Lydia Sellick, missionaries in the Republic of Panama. On
      occasion I accompanied him into the jungle and I can testify
      miraculous protection, where we experienced no ill effects
      from impure food and drink [not knowing what some of
      it was]. However, I carelessly shared a fine dinner in a very
      reputable home here in the U.S. and lost twenty pounds within
      24 hours, I was really sick; my wife and I prayed trusting God
      for my healing [I was healed in the name of Jesus]. The entire
      episode began and ended between Monday and Wednesday
      and I was able to lead the midweek services. These signs were
      given to encourage us to trust God, yet not to tempt Him with
      foolish experiments (see Mark 16:17-20; Acts 8:5-7; 19:12).
      Certainly all the glory and honor from these miracles go to
      God; because they are impossible for humankind to perform
      in their own strength.
    - *The blood of Jesus:* A genuine Christian is characterized by
      walking habitually in the light (truth and holiness) not in
      darkness (falsehood and sin). We have fellowship with one
      another and the blood of Jesus cleanses us from all sin; we are
      then fit for His use in supernatural power for service (see 1
      John 1:5-9; 3 John 11; James 1:27; Ephesians 5:11). The New
      Testament makes it clear that we must sprinkle the Blood of
      Jesus with faith and obedience. Many who claim to be under
      the Blood of Jesus are walking in deliberate disobedience. Peter
      gives some good teaching on this subject. We are "elect . . . unto

obedience and sprinkling of the blood of Jesus Christ" (1 Peter 1:2). In chapter 2, He continues the theme by telling us that we are holy priests to offer up spiritual sacrifices, acceptable to God by Jesus Christ (1 Peter 2:5). Think about how the destroyer, Satan (see Revelation 9:11), shied away from the blood sacrifices, and deliverances in the Old Testament; how much more should we honor the blood of Jesus. Let's look at Hebrews12:24 where we read that *"We are come to the blood of sprinkling."* This is a present tense experience. We also read, *"And they overcame him because of the blood of the Lamb and . . . the word of their testimony" (Revelation 12:11).*

- *The Word of God:* The Word of God is the absolute authority over our lives. As ministers of the gospel we are primarily a servant of God's Word, boldly and courageously sharing its message: *All Scripture is given by inspiration of God and is profitable for doctrine, for reproof, for correction, for instruction in righteousness, that the man of God may be complete, thoroughly equipped for every good work (2 Timothy 3:16, 17).* Paul is telling us here that the mature Christian will be enabled through the Word of God to meet all demands of godly ministry and righteous living (also see Ephesians 4:11-13). While the Word of God is comforting and nourishing to those who believe; it is a seed and has the power within to reproduce itself. It also has the power as a two-edged sword to expose those with shallow beliefs and false intentions (see Hebrews 4:12).

- *The promises of God:* Christ has made available to believers His exceedingly great and precious promises. The purpose of the promises is that we may be sharers of a deep spiritual union with Christ, and thereby enjoy the blessings and benefits of that relationship. Our inheritance as believers in Jesus Christ and His Word is a treasure of great worth. One of His promises gives insight into the inheritance we have already received: *"Blessed be the God and Father of our Lord Jesus Christ, who has blessed us with every spiritual blessing in the heavenly places in Christ" (Ephesians 1:3).*

God has already blessed us with all spiritual blessings in heavenly places in Christ! What a *promise* this is! It has already happened. Each of God's promises is a particular treasure in the inheritance we've received from God's hands. All spiritual blessings are already ours! It is important to know that each of these promises found almost on every page of the Bible are for us, God's children, to believe and receive (see Romans 8:28; Colossians 2:10; James 1:17; 2 Peter 1:3).

2. The second key is moving from fear to faith:

    •   Often I hear the leadership lamenting that the young people have no foundation or commitment on which to build their lives. Therefore, they are unstably moved by secular thought, while rejecting the truth of God's Word. The harsh reality is that the church is not very effective or skillful in reaching, training, and retaining young people. As a result, many are driven by fear and focus on worldly solutions and survival methods. Perhaps we should look at fear as faith in the devil. No young person wants to feel like they are on a sinking ship. It behooves us to stop focusing on survival and pursue revival. If this is going to happen we must begin to operate out of a deeper faith in the promises and power of God.

    •   Telling about the Lord's presence and power of God is not enough, we must help them to pursue it and operate in it through the building of strong Christian families. I am convinced that a community of Christian families makes a strong local church; which will provide stability, sustainability and spiritual growth. Christian growth comes through individual Bible study, personal prayer, and active participation in the corporate provision of one on one and small group development focused on purposeful relationships with other kingdom oriented individuals. This will help dispel the sense of apathy and irrelevance many of our young people feel toward their faith and church when facing culture shock upon leaving home. You cannot truly have an encounter with Jesus Christ and walk away at the same time!

3. The third key is to move from faith to trust:

    •   We must not only move from fear to faith, but from faith to trust. Trust involves *risk,* and *risky faith* is an essential component of the miraculous.
    •   Perhaps you are reading this and thinking this cannot possibly happen to you just because of who you are. God is no respecter of persons. Remember those known only as: the woman at the well, the woman with the issue of blood, the man who lay lame for 38 years, the centurion and others whom the Holy Spirit chose to record not by name, and yet God is glorified daily throughout the world by their modeled faith and trust in Him. Oh, what a blessing! I will expound further on these men and women who exercised risky faith under the next topic.

Miracles our inheritance

While I do not claim to be a faith-healer, on occasions God has wrought miracles through me. In my early pastoral experience a senior mother came forward as I invited people to come forward for prayer. She had been diagnosed with an incurable cancer. I was initially weakened in the knees by her condition and request; however I took the risk and as I prayed believing God would heal this mother, and praise God! He did! She claimed her healing while dancing in the Spirit around the sanctuary. As a result my faith increased and my unbelief decreased. God performed that miracle in 1982 she remains cancer free today as I am writing this book in 2011.

Since that day a number of others have been healed. All of us are capable of being used of God in healing and the supernatural if we are willing to *trust* God. Let's notice several examples of *individuals* who *trusted* Christ for their healing and other miracles:

And, behold, a woman which was diseased with an issue of blood twelve years, came behind him, and touched the hem of his garment: For she said within herself, If I may but touch his garment, I shall be whole. But Jesus turned about . . . he said, "Daughter, be of good comfort; thy faith hath made thee whole" (see Matthew 9:20-22 KJV).

Notice in this setting while there was a multitude present this *one* individual trusted Christ for her healing; and she got it! Praise God! Where is your faith on this scale? What risks have you taken for God? Move out into the deep! In another instance:

Jesus spake unto them, saying, Be of good cheer; it is I; be not afraid. And Peter answered him and said, Lord, if it be thou, bid me come unto thee on the water. And he said, Come. And when Peter was come down out of the ship, he walked on the water, to go to Jesus (see Matthew 14:27-29 KJV).

Again, *one* individual took the risk and trusted Jesus for a miracle. While all twelve disciples no doubt had great faith; eleven remained on board, as only one trusted Jesus and walked on the water. If the other disciples would have stepped out and followed Peter's lead I'm sure that the Holy Spirit would have reported it here. Are you trusting Christ for your miracle?

Then Mark in chapter 9:25-29 records the story of the man bringing his son to the disciples desiring that he be healed of a dumb spirit. The disciples could not do it. Jesus said to him, if you can believe, all things are possible. The father cried out, Lord I believe; *help my unbelief.* Jesus then, cast the spirit out of the boy. Here we see another factor introduced concerning our faith. Unbelief! In both the case of the disciples and the father, they had faith but it seems their faith was counteracted by their unbelief. The Scripture says, *"God hath dealt to every man the measure of faith"* (Romans 12:3 KJV).

I have queried my students about unbelief; it seems few want to admit that they have unbelief. The father in the Scripture above admitted to Jesus that he had both faith and unbelief. Jesus told the disciples that they could not cast out the demon because of their unbelief (see Matthew 17:20). Unbelief is very subtle and one of Satan's most dependable weapons. Many people pray, fast and cry out to God for more faith, when it's their unbelief they should be dealing with.

As I stated earlier many do not want to identify with unbelief; knowing that unbelief negates faith; and then there are those who accept it as a normal part of life. Unbelief must be annihilated by God; however, you will never be delivered of it until you confess your need of deliverance, humble yourself and seek the Lord's help. Unbelief is a stronghold or mindset that leads you to believe that becoming like Christ is impossible.

Strongholds are thoughts built into us through our experiences and the conclusions we have drawn from them and for better or for worse they are what we call reality. God defines reality as truth. When we come to Christ in regeneration; He empowers and directs us through diligent study of the Word of God and the Holy Spirit. Our thinking must change. The Scripture admonishes, *"and be renewed in the spirit of your mind; and that you put on the new man, which after God is created in righteousness and true holiness" (see Ephesians 4:23-24).* In order to recognize what is wrong in us, we must pursue God's standard of right. The promise of God is: *"If any man be in Christ, he is a new creature; the old things passed away; behold new things have come" (2 Corinthians 5:17).* Please believers, take this personal. Everything even your intelligence and physical appearance is now subject to change for the better; therefore your old prejudices, failures, and attitudes are destined to go and new faith and hope should be growing within you daily. How do we attain such a new beginning? Again, Christ in our hearts to empower us!

PERSONAL JOURNAL NOTES
(REFLECTION & RESPONSE)

1. The most important thing I learned from this chapter was:

2. The area that I need to work on the most is:

3. I can apply this lesson to my life by:

4. Closing statement of Commitment

CHAPTER ELEVEN

Carnality is the enemy of the Soul

When I was growing up, at every turn people were concerned with winning souls to Christ. Today, concern for the salvation of souls, seems to be waning along with the requirements of virtues and godly living. Many ministers and ministries seem to have shifted from soul winning to prosperity and healing, thus leaving many people seeking prosperity and healing without being born again, the first work. It is error to lead people to believe they can get to God and His grace another way. Jesus said, "Seek first the kingdom of God and His righteousness and these other things will be added" (see Matthew 6:33). That's God's order of priority. His will is that none should perish. However, that means salvation His way (see 2 Corinthians 5:17, 21). My premise throughout this book deals with Satan's deception that says, God's way through the precious blood of Jesus Christ is only one of many ways to God. God forbid!

Many are falling for Satan's lie because it promises a life that does not require such virtues as integrity, commitment, accountability, faithfulness, and righteousness as the standards of living. At the center of the Christian life is the expectation of moral excellence and godliness. So many reject these standards because they feel that it's impossible for them to live such a life; and truthfully they can't in themselves. However, God's plan guarantees for those in Christ another Helper. Jesus told His disciples, *"And I will pray the Father, and He will give you another Helper that He may abide with you forever—the Spirit of truth, whom the world cannot receive, because it neither sees Him nor knows Him; but you know Him; for He dwells with you and will be in you. I will not leave you orphans, I will come to you" (John 14:16-18).*

All three members of the Trinity are mentioned here. Jesus prayed to the Father who would give the Holy Spirit (forever). Jesus said, "I will come to you" (v. 18). In this same chapter, Philip asks Jesus to show them the Father. Jesus answers Him, "He who has seen Me has seen the Father. Do you not believe that I am in the Father and the Father in Me?" (see vv. 9, 10). Jesus preceded this wonderful promise with, *"If"* coming before *"and I will"* above. *"If you love Me, keep My commandments" (v. 15).* Jesus goes on to say in verse 20, *"At that day you will know that I am in My Father and you in Me, and I in you."*

What Jesus is making clear is the fact that He is alive and living in the believer in the Person of the Holy Spirit (see John 16:16). We see the difference in His disciples after Pentecost. So these verses conclude Jesus' answer to Philip's request, "show us the Father" in (v. 8).

Loving Jesus Christ finds its most comprehensive expression in obeying His commandments, which are also the Father's commandments. Those other ways satisfied with less commitment may be convenient, but is too cheap to be biblical. Jesus promised to manifest Himself in the believer who keeps His commandments. The Greek term used here *"emphanidzo;"* Strong's #1718: a combination of *en,* "in" and *phaino,* means *"to cause to shine,"* thus, to appear, come into view, reveal, exhibit, make visible, present oneself to the sight of another, be conspicuous. So emphanidzo is the self-revelation of Jesus to believers. Know that you show your love for Jesus Christ by obeying Him. Diligently keep God's Word so that His presence will steadfastly abide in you.

Loving God's Word

Jesus completely aligned His life and will with the Father's (see John 8:29), which indicates His total allegiance to the Father's *Word* and *commandments.* He also said He disapproved of any attitude that would reduce respect for or teach less than full obedience to the entirety of God's revealed Word (see Matthew 5:17-19). In this text then, when He explicitly links His disciples' love for Him as Savior with their will to keep His commandments, we conclude Jesus' clear intent: If we love Him, we will love the Father's Word also.

Our Lord declares that the *knowledge* of the Scriptures is the pathway to *knowing Him well!* (see John 5:39). Further, upon His resurrection, He unveiled the fullness of His own Person. Luke reports, *"And beginning at Moses and all the Prophets, He expounded to them in all the Scriptures the things concerning Himself" (see Luke 24:27).* The problem of those, whom Jesus was addressing in this passage were suffering from the same malady as so many Christians today: *spiritual dullness, coming from a failure to recognize that the Scriptures foretold the necessity of Jesus Christ's shed blood. The Scriptures not only prophesy the death and resurrection of the Messiah, but decree that the redemptive message is to be offered to all nations (see Luke 24:47).*

Spiritual Wisdom

The Spirit answers to spirit, and not to the mind. We should recognize that the natural mind cannot understand or receive from the Holy Spirit. The Holy Spirit reveals spiritual things to spiritual people. Paul elaborates on our need of the Holy Spirit-given wisdom and revelation, and he firmly combines this with our receiving the "words . . . Which the Holy Spirit teaches us (see 1 Corinthians 2:13). In applying this true wisdom to *practical* life, there is a part to be played by the believers themselves (see vv. 6-9) and a part to be played by the Holy Spirit (see vv.10-13).

In the doctrinal passage (1 Corinthians 1:18-2:16), Paul immediately condemns the false wisdom in the natural world around him, and unfortunately in the church also. He drew a contrast between that and the true wisdom of God. God's wisdom humbles human pride (see 1 Corinthians 1:27-31).The Greeks frequently determined status by intellectual attainment, measured by the academic titles and honors that the world bestowed upon the eloquent.

The roots of the false wisdom of the Corinthians were attributed to their shallow intake of God's Word. The demanding truth of this passage is that no amount of supposed insight or experience reflects genuine spiritual growth, *if it is separated from our basic growth in the knowledge of God's Word in the Bible.* Without being rooted in the Word of God, we may be deceived concerning our spiritual growth. These roots are in truth and love, not merely a cognitive exercise of learning knowledge or some accomplished study. In all cases, believers must recognize that true wisdom begins with *God's revelation,* never with human efforts to arrive at the truth (see 1 Corinthians 2:9); this requires our diligently spending time in the Word and separating ourselves from the hindrances of lovelessness, competitiveness, and strife. Once the believer submits to the authority of divine revelation, the Holy Spirit takes it upon Himself to provide the illumination necessary to understand it.

Three Spiritual Categories

In 1 Corinthians 3:1-7, Paul identifies three categories of people in the local church. The ground gained by these various groups has changed tremendously. Many churches today have met their spiritual demise as they strived to be inclusive in church membership; which leads to division, as happened in Corinth. Instead the church should seek to follow Christian unity in Christ, unlike the people who wanted to follow the Apollos Party, Cephas Party, Paul Party, or the Christ Party.

It's sad to say that asking about a born again experience or other spiritual experiences are antiquated today in many local church settings. Questions like "Do you believe in God" or "What do you bring to the church?" What they mean is profession or talent. If answered in the affirmative they receive a hardy, "Welcome to the body of Christ!" As we look at these groups, notice only one third of them has a clear revelation of the cross and necessity of the shed blood of Christ. These three categories are the natural man, the carnal man, and the spiritual man:

- *The natural man,* unregenerate and devoid of the Spirit, has no appreciation for the gospel; nor ability to receive the special wisdom of the Spirit of God since he or she has not acquired the new birth (see 2:14).
- A *carnal Christian,* must be fed with "milk" and not with "solid food" (see 3:2), so therefore he or she will not find the wisdom of the Holy Spirit attained only by Spiritual Christians.
- A *spiritual Christian,* through spirituality has received the wisdom of the Holy Spirit and the solution to their problem of divisions. This wisdom comes *not* through further academic training or even through more doctrinal teaching, but rather through *deeper sanctification, a closer walk with Jesus Christ.*

The Solution

Paul's solution to the wisdom problem involves three suggestions to the Corinthians:

1. *Strive for wider cooperation among Christians (see 3:5-9).* Paul and Apollos worked together and were of one mind. Paul, who sowed the seed in Corinth, was happy to have Apollos water it (3:6). Both rejoiced when God gave the increase. It did not make sense to them that the Corinthians would organize parties around their names as a basis for splitting the church. If they had followed their leaders' example they would have worked in cooperation rather than in conflict. Paul admonishes them to forget about the four parties and get together.

What does this mean for us today? There are two major differences between the twenty-first century church and the Corinthian church. The first difference is that Paul faced a united church which had just begun to split. Today we face a long-divided church making major efforts to unite. However, many of these efforts appear to be based on interpretation, programs and attitudes just as carnal as those underlying the Corinthian splits. Christians must be watchful and aware of carnality wherever it is operative.

The second difference is that many of today's divisions are caused by moral issues. Coming together does not involve a simple change of attitude in many instances, but rather a change of world view. For instance, on the evening news yesterday a major denominational church announced to the world that the church voted not to perform any marriages until same sex marriages are permitted. True Christians must always be willing to enter dialogue with each other trusting the Spirit of God to lead both to a Biblical position.

2. *Have full confidence in the work of the Holy Spirit (3:16, 17).* Once another person is born again, he or she enjoys the ministry of the Holy Spirit in their heart just as we do. It is presumptuous to jump to the conclusion that any one Christian can have a corner on the Holy Spirit. God is not a respecter of persons. He may be able to lead my brother or sister better than He is leading me. Sometimes this

is hard to accept, but to do so is a sure sign of Christian maturity. If such an attitude of true humility penetrated the Church on all levels, problems of division would soon disappear.

3. Finally, Paul suggests to the Corinthians that they *stop judging their brother in Christ* (see 3:10-15, 18-21). Paul inserts the passage on the Judgment Seat of Christ to remind the Corinthians that each Christian is responsible before God for his or her own acts. Since God will judge each individual according to his or her works, Christians should stop taking upon themselves God's prerogative of judgment. Paul exhorts, *"So do not pass premature judgment before the Lord comes" (see 5:5)*. How to handle church divisions? Look behind whatever superficial reasons given and locate the carnality that certainly is there. Carnal Christians with their worldly attitudes are always behind divisions in the church. Each of us has the responsibility to heal the divisions and strive to prevent the occurrence of new ones. Carnality plays funny tricks. Notice the Corinthian church, divided when they were supposed to be united, and they remained united when they were supposed to be divided.

The great deception of carnality

In chapters 5 and 6 of First Corinthians, Paul faces a different challenge, but once again carnality is the cause. A member of the church was in an adulterous affair with his stepmother (see 5:1). Years ago I read a book titled, "The Silent Issues of the Church." Though this particular sin was not listed in it then; I am sure that if that book was revised today this immorality would certainly top its list. To be more specific adultery and fornication consistently appear at the top of the major lists of sins in the New Testament. Today this sin has probably doubled, and tops the *silent* issues list. With slight variation Paul's problem in Corinth is viewed about the same in many American churches today.

There were some standards in Corinth incest was even frowned on by the non-Christians. Paul says that this sin was *"a kind which does not occur among the Gentiles" (see 5:1)*. Here a sin even shunned by the unbelievers had invaded the church! Although the sin shocked Paul deeply, it was not the most serious trouble. Here we have double trouble! Even worse than this sin, was the apparent attitude of the whole congregation toward the sin. *"And you, rather than grieving about it enough to remove the person who committed such a deed, are you puffed up?" (5:2).*

Here is the major deception of carnality that is so prevalent in the churches today; brought to us by the Corinthian church of the first century. Because of it, the believers had allowed *pride* to creep into their hearts concerning the matter. In (5:6), Paul labels it *"boasting."* What could they be proud of? Certainly they were not boasting that they had a case of incest in their church. Rather, their pride undoubtedly centered in their concept of *"tolerance."* Truly there is nothing new under the sun! The leadership probably expressed:

- What the brother does in his private life is entirely his business.
- He tithes his income, attends church regularly and he keeps the golden rule.
- Furthermore this affair with his step-mother is probably a meaningful relationship for both of them.
- It's not good that we be pharisaical about this.
- Our obligation is to continue to love him (notice who is missing here).

Undoubtedly excommunicating the brother was never a consideration of the leadership in this case, just excuse him. This carnal attitude is sweeping this deception through our churches today. This new tolerance may be a pleasing characteristic in secular circles, but when it is used to excuse immorality in the church, it is definitely error. In his response, Paul compares the sin of the Corinthian church with leaven; therefore, the only thing you can do with the old leaven is purge it out (5:7). Paul insisted on strict discipline! The church is therefore, to remove everything sinful in order to be separate from the old life, including the influence of sinful church members. The church is to be in the world, but not of the world.

When tolerated, sin will permeate and corrupt the whole church. The Scripture informs us that Satan has the power to appear as an angel of light; this being true undoubtedly he has empowered his ministers and children to do the same. Watch and pray for your churches beginning with the pulpits! Not to apply discipline when necessary reflects carnality in the church, this case can be taken as an example. Perhaps many of us should re-examine our own congregations to see if failure to follow this biblical precept isn't the reason for the lack of power and the exodus of members from our local churches today.

Just as unleavened bread symbolized being freed from Egypt, by the Passover (see Exodus 12:15-17)), so the church is to be unleavened, since it has been separated from the dominion of sin and death by the shed blood of our perfect Passover Lamb, the Lord Jesus Christ.

PERSONAL JOURNAL NOTES
(REFLECTION & RESPONSE)

1. The most important thing I learned from this chapter is:

2. the area that I need to work on the most is:

3. I can apply this lesson to my life by:

4. Closing statement of commitment:

CHAPTER TWELVE

WHEN TRIALS COME

"Gird up the loins of your mind, be sober,
and rest your hope fully upon the grace
that is to be brought to you
at the revelation of Jesus Christ" (1 Peter 1:13).

Faith in the Person of Christ and in His finished work on the cross allows a Christian to endure rejection from the world. The word "gird up" is similar to fasten your seat belts and get ready for take off; we expect to encounter turbulence and severe storms on the journey—but nothing is too hard for our pilot, Jesus Christ! This turbulence or rejection is intensifying as the world through biblical ignorance get bolder in their hatred for Christ and the Children of God. Peter advises Christians to be obedient to God's Word and be not conformed to the old life. In other words don't you be ignorant and not heed the call of God to be holy in all of your conduct, because it is written, *"Be holy for I am holy."*

Commit yourself to God

The word for "commit" used in this instance is a banking term; it refers to the act of leaving an amount on deposit for safekeeping.

Knowing that you were not redeemed with corruptible things, like
silver or gold, from your aimless conduct received by tradition
from your fathers, but with the precious blood if Christ,
as a lamb without blemish and without spot (1 Peter 1:18-19).

Here in (vv. 18-19), Peter continues to concern himself with trials. Peter's argument in these verses should be our plea today. As Christians, we must be mindful of the fact that you were not redeemed (bought back) through those old earthly ways inherited from your fathers; but only through Christ, the ultimate Lamb, who is offered in our place to pay the price for our sins. So don't conform to Rome! He urged them to commit themselves to Christ whose precious blood had provided their salvation. Certainly his plea is just as applicable to all believers today as it was to the first century believers.

Roman law required each citizen to pledge his or her loyalty to the emperor. The citizens were commanded to put a portion of incense on their idolatrous altar and say, "Caesar is lord!"(see 1 Peter 3:15). Instead of obeying Rome, the Christians refused to bow to Caesar and confessed "Jesus Christ is Lord!" This resulted in their persecution, arrest, and into fiery trials that reaped certain death for many of them.

When trials come, we are suffering for Jesus' sake and sharing in His suffering. Daily more and more home Bible studies are being harassed and in many cases outlawed in some places across America. Preaching and teaching truth today invites these new tolerance critics. I am committed to truth. In these changing times blood-washed Christians have no other choice! But take heart! I received an e-mail concerning a couple being fined $300 for conducting a Bible study in their home in California. History reflects that more people have died for the cause of Christ in the past century than all other periods combined. The suffering we endure now is but a taste to the glory that we will share at His coming. When Daniel was in the lion's den, God preserved and delivered him (see Daniel 6:1-28).

While we read about various fiery trials of the saints around the world, we seem oblivious of such things happening here in the United States. While it may not seem newsworthy and therefore goes under reported by the secular media, we find that Christians are being persecuted here in America. Many cases are reported wherein Christians are losing their jobs, being denied employment, the butt of jokes, ridiculed, shunned, and physically attacked in some cases for the cause of Christ. If we are not careful new church sites will be non existent because they will be outlawed through zoning boards.

I am a collector of caps. I have some with Christian logos, professional emblems and some from service organizations. I have three favorites I wear from time to time just to gauge public reaction. On the front of one is the American flag. I receive smiles, nods and even some salutes. Another one has a fish and the words "I'd rather be fishing." Certainly, many even strangers strike up friendly conversations on that subject. However, on occasion I wear my third favorite with "Man of Faith" a cross and Bible on the front. All three caps carry a message, but this particular cap seems to offend some people! Just "Man of Faith" without the cross and Bible would probably be acceptable since faith is so broadly defined today. I purposely wear it sometimes while transacting business or on appointments interacting with people. Reactions vary sometimes I'm stared at, glared at, but certainly waited on promptly. Over the past two years I have seen on the faces of people and felt the tension of rejection in crowds.

We submit ourselves to God as we obey His Word. This is a daily submission, living to please Him and serve others. This is the tragedy of many churches, so little evidence of true Christianity. Biblical teaching and training are replaced by some uninspired program; written in many cases by secular authors. Therefore, their solutions to crisis and other problems are secularly oriented. God forbid! I preached a sermon some years ago, titled "All of The Devil's Apples Have Worms." My argument was, the apple with the hole could be safer to eat than the one without. The reason being if there is a hole, the worm has bored its way out. How did he get there if not through the hole? The apple with the worm is whole without a hole. The worm contamination was placed on the blossom and as the blossom grew into an apple the larvae developed and grew inside of it, then eventually the worm bore its way out. Some may be so embedded that when you do discover them, it's too late!

The individual is contaminated with sin at conception. We are all born in sin and shaped in iniquity because that worm grew and developed in our original parents, Adam and Eve. We have means today to eradicate that worm (sin) through planting the counter Seed, Jesus Christ, into our children's hearts; therefore developing an enduring biblical worldview giving them a stable early devotional life. Teaching the Word of God by mouth and example insures proper spiritual growth through the Holy Spirit. Sin already has a jump on our children since they are born with it; however, we can interrupt its development through an early rebirth. I have baptized children age 4 years and up. However parental involvement is essential because this process begins in the womb. If we think little boyfriends and girlfriends are cute and even encouraged at four, how much more should we be concerned about their early spiritual development?

Commit your children to God

Before conception the parents can determine what the child will be by simply following the example of Hannah (see 1 Samuel 2:1, 21). She prayed for a child and promised God that she would give the child back to Him; then followed through with the promise after the child, the great prophet Samuel, was born.

During my many years as pastor, I've seen so many young rising stars go out because they were not properly trained and oriented by the parents and the church concerning the facts of life. Over the years, my wife and I have taken in a number of young girls (for a period of time) who were literally put out of the home by their parents. In most cases the reason for this abusive act was due to the child's conduct hurting their pride and standing in the church or community. Undoubtedly the welfare of the girls was not considered a priority.

Jesus is the Master teacher. A woman was brought to Him who was caught in the very act of sinning. He did not condemn her, but forgave her. His stern counsel to her, *"Go and sin no more"* (see John 8:11). That's love! The news media reports stories daily of our youths going off the deep end and, not surviving because of a lack of love on the part of the parent (s) or significant others. One of the best examples of parent/ child rearing is the eagle and eaglet. Eagles were created to fly and survive in the world. When that time comes the eaglet is not just thrown out of the nest and told something like, "you're on your own now." Don't come back here if you have a problem. I can barely make it myself." No, the parent eagle puts briers in the bottom of the nest which makes it uncomfortable over time as the cushioning materials wear out.

One day due to the eaglet's growth and the nest is no longer comfortable. The eaglet is pushed out, but under the watchful eye of the parent eagle. The eaglet struggles to fly but continues to fall; all a part of the necessary training. The parent swoops down and lifts the eaglet on her wings safely back to the nest. This training continues and one day while the eaglet falls; it begins to flap its wings and notices a lift and soon it soars. "I can fly!"

We are the high point of God's creation. We were created in His image. Yet, the lower animal kingdom can teach us much because what God has given us to prepare our eaglets in many cases is never used. We were made to soar like the eagles! I find eagles fascinating because of their strength and survival skills. Their ability to soar allows them to rise above some storms. However, God also created them with special eyelids to protect their eyes, and with their strength and toughness they fly directly through other storms. They have extraordinary vision which enables them to spot fish in streams from as much as 4 or 5 miles up or away. We've already noted that they teach their young to fly. I'm sure that before they are on their own the parent eagles have given them the skills and knowledge necessary for a long life.

As parents, we need to know what our role is for the benefit of our children, to help teach them and let them know they can rely on us as they grow toward independence. Often we focus on what we want our children to do for us. Without quoting statistics this problem is prevalent through out society. It has been said, "When all is said and done, children are nothing more than an extension of the parents' egos!" I'm sure that many of us find this statement to be offensive. But it is true in the sense that many of us never consider what is best for the child rather than what would satisfy my pride.

A good parent views his or her child as a person, as a feeling, thinking individual, with God's image, not as a possession. The parent must be the foundational example (see II Timothy 3:15; Proverbs 22:6). Conversely, children whose parents live righteously produce off springs that do likewise. These same principles pertain to young converts. We must instill in them that our loving heavenly Father assumes their care forever! We should live so as to say to our children,

> *"My son, give me your heart*
> *and let your eyes observe*
> *and delight in my ways"*
> *(Proverbs 23:26 Amplified Bible).*

How we live as parents equals the kind of children we will turn out. If our children are not developing spiritually and morally as they should, it does not mean there is something wrong with them but it indicates a lack in our parenting. Forget the old clichés, "preachers' kids are the worse kids" etc, etc." As a general rule children become what the parents allow them to become (preachers, doctors, mechanics, waiters, computer operators or what). Think of Noah's example. I heard a preacher say that Noah's preaching for 120 years with only eight souls saved was a failure. Let's see how God viewed the situation. In Genesis 6:9 He says, Noah was a just man, perfect in his generations. Noah walked with God. In verse 22 we read, Thus Noah did; according to all that God commanded him, so he did. No doubt God was pleased with the fruit of Noah's labor for in Genesis 7:13, we see that those saved were his very own family.

Again, Noah obeyed the Lord fully (see Genesis 7:5). Isn't it interesting, when we stand before the Lord all of our temporal earthly possessions will have perished; however every child that we have conceived in this world will have to be accounted for? We must give account for anything else that is not under the blood of Jesus. What will we tell Him?

Christ is our righteousness

In chapter 10 of Romans, Paul explains why Israel is in its present spiritual condition as a nation. Key in this chapter is the word "righteousness." The Jews wanted righteousness, but on their own terms. Like the Pharisees described in Matthew 23:15; the Jews put forth much effort in securing a right standing before God, their deeds were done in ignorance. The Pharisees were the top level religious leaders of their day; and yet they rejected Christ in spite all of the evidence. Many church leaders and parents worldwide are making the same tragic choices with their converts and children respectively as these Pharisees, with the same results.

It's such a sad commentary today, as in Jesus' day much of today's rejection is led by the religious elite. They think that God will accept them for their good works. The Bible speaks of *two* kinds of righteousness that corresponds with the so-called two ways to God and heaven:

- "Works righteousness," which comes from obeying the law, (the natural).
- "Faith righteousness," which is the gift of God to those who trust His Son, (the spiritual).

The Jews would not submit to faith righteousness; their religious pride turned them away from simple saving faith to *(another way)*, blind religion! As we approach the end of the end times please notice, the problem of people thinking there is another way to God other than the substitutionary death of Jesus Christ in their place. They have rejected Christ and clung to the Law. Please note several practical points:

- Salvation is not difficult: *"Whosoever shall call upon the name of the Lord shall be saved" (Romans 10:11).*
- It is important that the Word of God be presented to the lost sinners. It is the Word that convicts, that gives faith, and leads to life in Christ.
- There are only two "religions" (practice of beliefs) in the world: works-righteousness and faith-righteousness. Nobody can fulfill the first, but praise God everybody can respond to the second. The blood runs through it!

One of my foundational favorite verses of Scripture is 2 Corinthians 5:21,

> *For He made Him who knew no sin*
> *to be sin for us,*
> *that we might become*
> *the righteousness of God in Him."*

This verse is the positive counterpart to the statement in v. 19 that God does not impute our trespasses to *us*. He imputed them instead to Christ, who was sinless in every respect (see Hebrews 4:15; 1 Peter 2:22; 1 John 3:5).He bore our sins on the Cross and endured the penalty that we deserved. He becomes our Savior. It is a personal experience!

Knowledge is essential

In our regeneration the Holy Spirit quickens our spirit which was dead as the result of sin:

(1) We heard the gospel and positively responded to it by repentance toward God and faith in Jesus Christ (see Romans 10:9-10).

(2) For a clearer understanding (spiritual growth) of what salvation is as defined by Jesus Himself, notice what He says in John 17:3, *"And this is life eternal, that they may know You, the only true God, and Jesus Christ whom You have sent."* It is not enough simply to know about Jesus Christ, we must know Him personally. The apostle Paul expresses it this way, *"that I may know Him and the power of His resurrection, and the fellowship of His sufferings, being conformed to His death."*

(3) In regeneration we must remember, it is our spirit that is reborn; as the soul and body must be renewed. In his second epistle, Peter warns Christians against false teachers within their fellowship who would lead them into apostasy. Fidelity to the Holy Spirit and the Scriptures then and now are the main concerns (see especially 1 Peter1:12-16; 3:1, 2, 15, 16).

(4) The soul which comprise the mind, emotions, and will must be renewed through growing in the knowledge of the Lord (cultivating spiritual maturity). Peter further explains, *"As His divine power has given to us all things that pertain to life and godliness, through the knowledge of Him who called us by glory and virtue"* (2 Peter 1:3). Virtue signifies intrinsic value, moral excellence and godliness.

(5) In 2 Peter 1:4, we are given the definition of a Christian as a *"partaker of the divine nature."* He goes on to say in essence faith in the Person of Christ and His completed work of the Cross allows a Christian to endure rejection of the world. This rejection may lead to death. The faith-filled Christian glorifies God and counts it a blessing to stand for the Lord. Such a stand for Christ is preceded by the denial of fleshly lust so that the Spirit is in control (see vv. 5-8).

(6) Hebrews 4:12 tell us, *"For the word of God is living and powerful, and sharper than any two-edged sword, piercing even to the division of soul and spirit, and of joints and marrow, and is a discerner of the thoughts and intents of the heart.* Hearing the Word regenerates and

redeems. Man is made in the image of God: *"And God said, Let us make man in OUR image, after OUR likeness . . ." (see Genesis 1:26).* God is a trinity, and therefore man is a trinity—spirit, soul, and body. As stated earlier, the spirit is the highest part of man. It is the spirit that makes man God-conscious and capable of worshiping Him.

While the writings of preachers and teachers can help us better understand the Bible, only the Bible can impart life to the soul and renew it to its proper alignment in God's order of spirit, soul, and body (see 1 Thessalonians 5:23). The soul or flesh does not give up *its stolen position* without a fight! The unregenerate person is dominated by his or her soul, remember the unregenerate can only walk in the flesh (see 1 Corinthians 2:14). To that person, spiritual things are foolishness and he or she can never know the things of God until the Holy Spirit quickens (bring to life) the spirit in regeneration and that person comes to know "the eternal power of the Godhead." We read in 1 Corinthians 15:45, *"And so it is written, the first man Adam was made a living soul; the last Adam was made a quickening spirit." "The first man is of the earth, earthy; the second Man is the Lord from heaven" (1 Corinthians 15:47).*

I repeat, we are born again by the power of the Word of God (see Romans 1:16, 17; John 5:24; Ephesians 2:8; Romans 10:17). We are saved by hearing and receiving the Word of God, and when we receive the Word, it literally *"divides asunder"* soul and spirit. Thus we are *reconciled to God* (see II Corinthians 5:19) through our born again spirit which returns to the place of communion with God which Adam had before he sinned.

Christians rest by faith in the finished work of the Lord Jesus Christ. We labor, pressing toward the mark of the prize of the high calling of God in Christ Jesus, pressing on to that incorruptible inheritance reserved in heaven for us; and while traveling through this world we are guided by the Holy Spirit and the Word of God. We have the Word to encourage us; it is a lamp to our feet and a light to our pathway.

It is no wonder the devil is doing all in his power today to discredit the Word of God through anyone who will listen to him. He is seeking to rob the Word of its verbal inspiration and power. The Word is declared to be endowed with all the attributes of Almighty God Himself and truly, *"In the beginning was the Word, and the Word was with God, and the Word WAS God . . . and the Word was made flesh . . ." (John 1:1, 14).*

The Word of God is a mirror that brings us into the very presence of the Holy God who desires truth in the inward man. The Christian who abides in the Word is judged, chastened, corrected, led, and rebuked. Such a believer cries out with David, "Search me O God, and know my heart: try me, and know my thoughts: and see if there is any wicked way in me, and lead me in the way everlasting" (Psalm 139:23, 24). This believer finds peace surpassing all understanding and without the conviction, the chastening, and correction that comes through diligent, untiring study and meditation of the Word, there can be no complete peace and rest in Christ.

Very few Christians enjoy their spiritual birthright because they do not study diligently to show themselves approved unto God, looking into the mirror of the perfect law of liberty, the Word of the living God.

Personal Journal Notes (Reflection & Response)

1. The most important thing I learned from this chapter was:

2. The area that I need to work on the most is:

3. I can apply this lesson to my life by:

4. Closing statement of Commitment:

CHAPTER THIRTEEN

Spiritual Warfare

During the Vietnam War, after fighting a major battle and winning the victory, our main forces would move on to the next objective. Left behind would be a small detachment of men whose task was to do what we called "mop up." In other words though the battle is over there is some resistance left in the populace: sympathizers, booby trap setters, mines, and even some surviving enemy soldiers to be dwelt with. Though the big flash and bang of war had passed, this was not a time to let down your guard. Remaining vigilant and alert during mop up operations is imperative because the enemy's goal remains to do you bodily or psychological harm.

Another problem we encountered was how easily the enemy could attack us then blend right back into the populace. Many who walked among us by day became casualties of war as they attacked us by night. That popular saying, "One man's trash is another man's treasure" was certainly true in Vietnam. A c-ration can, old nails, bottles, and just about anything that we carelessly threw away became the enemies' treasure as he sent it back to us the next day in a homemade bomb, booby trap or some other simple delivery.

Guerilla warfare was new to many of us, because most of our training at that time was based on World War II and the Korean War era tactics. During those encounters there was a marked line of defense; but here no lines. One secluded enemy soldier could wreck havoc on a careless team and kill you! It takes time to root out and destroy these pockets of resistance. You know the victory has been won; but you had to remain alert, prepared and always expecting the unexpected. Some of these small battles required more firepower than the mop up team's capabilities, so we had to send out a call for heavier weapons support.

War in the Christian's Life

In the Christian life, we know that the battle for our souls was won by our Lord and Savior, Jesus Christ on Calvary. Satan is defeated! Christ stripped him of all he took from Adam. However, the "mock up battle" now rages in our minds. Our minds are the conduits through which we think and are swayed negatively or positively in our decision making processes. We are all born with a conscious enabling us to know right from wrong; however, sin marred the conscious rendering it untrustworthy, alone. In fact you can turn the conscious on and off like a light switch.

Unless you are born again, Satan puts forth tremendous effort to keep you unsaved since he has full access to your mind and therefore he is very present and influential in your life decisions, conduct and behavior. While many unsaved are good moral people, the fact that they are unsaved means that they share Adam's sin nature; which all of humanity is born with. It is the nature of the birds to sing, dogs to bark, cats to meow, and humans to sin. Unless each individual turns to God in regeneration there is no hope for him or her coming to God in this world or the world to come. However, there is good news and hope for the sinner! Keep reading!

The Scripture says, *"That if you confess with your mouth the Lord Jesus and believe in your heart that God has raised Him from the dead, you will be saved. For with the heart one believes unto righteousness, and with the mouth confession is made unto salvation" (Romans 10:9-10).* Confessing that Jesus is God and Lord of all creation is not a simple nod of acknowledgment, since even demons acknowledge that to be true (see James 2:19). It is imperative for salvation that you believe that God raised Jesus from the dead, because it proved that He was who He claimed to be.

Just as the sunset serves as a demarcation line between day and night, the Resurrection of Jesus Christ clearly divides Him from the rest of humanity, proving without a shadow of a doubt that He is the Son of God and that the Father had accepted His sacrifice in the place of sinners (see Romans 4:24; Acts 13:32-33; 1 Peter 1:3-4). Without Christ's death and resurrection, there is no salvation (see 1 Corinthians 15:14-17). The person who repents and confesses Jesus as Lord, in agreement with the Father's declaration that Jesus is Savior and Lord is saved. For even Christ, our Passover is sacrificed for us (see1 Corinthians 5:7).

Walk in the Spirit

Jesus is not just our Savior, He is the Indwelling One who fulfills God's eternal purpose, to conform us to His image, the firstborn of a family of glorious sons (see Hebrews 2:10; Romans 8:28-29). The essence of our thought life is who we really are (see Proverbs 23:7). Therefore we are admonished to be renewed in the spirit of our minds; and that we put on the new man, which after God is created in righteousness and true holiness (see Ephesians 4:23-24). Listen to this promise:

> *Therefore, if anyone is in Christ,*
> *he is a new creation; old things have passed away,*
> *behold, all things*
> *have become new (2 Corinthians 5:17).*

After a person is saved or regenerated, old value systems, priorities, beliefs, loves and plans are gone. Evil and sin are still present, but the new believer sees them in a new perspective. Christ in me is my hope of glory! The believer's new spiritual perception of everything is now a constant reality for those who live for eternal not temporal things. Like their salvation, the believer's sanctification and good works were ordained before the foundation of the world (see James 2:14-25; Ephesians 2:10).

In Romans 8:1, we have the promise that there is no condemnation to those who are in Christ Jesus, who do not walk according to the flesh, but according to the Spirit. *"Glory to glory" (see 2 Corinthians 3:18).* What is your part in this? Renew your minds through diligent study of God's Word; and fail not to assemble yourselves with other saints (see Hebrews 10:25). A line from a little children's song says, "Read your Bible and pray everyday, and you'll grow, grow, grow!" The devil is not happy about your decision to serve the Lord. Of course anything that he tries to throw at you will only make you stronger in the Lord. God's faithfulness is His promises to us.

What we Face

Before we engage any enemy, certainly we would want to know everything that we can about them. Warfare is a life or death situation. Neither Satan nor his demons can possess you now that you are a child of God, however, he will try to win your mind and through it control your soul. Get it into your heart, *"Greater is He that is in you than he that is in the world" (1 John 4:4).* Later you'll really see what this verse means to you as a Christian. Here is some very important information you should know about Satan:

- He is an ancient and extremely treacherous foe. The apostle Peter speaks of him as a roaring lion going about seeking whom he may devour. Satan deceives many today who do not study our field manual, the Bible; therefore they are ignorant of his deceptive tactics. To Peter he is a lion in the street.

- On the other hand the strength of most Christians is primarily in idealism and untested fervor or zeal. The apostle John clarifies that when he speaks of Satan; in the church as a slithering serpent. Picture him as you sit in the pew, there near you ready to strike. We arc not speaking of flesh and blood serpents, but much worse, false teachers, who have slithered into the assembly energized by Satan and walking among us as angels of light. Now rather than the roar of a lion there is the slick tongued hiss of the serpent!

- Satan attacks and we are defeated! What happened? Zeal challenged the treachery of hell and lost. Don't leave for battle too soon! The first consideration in spiritual warfare is *wisdom.* Wisdom provides stability to prevent Christians from being tossed to and fro during this crucial period of cultural and religious challenge. Hear the Word of God:

> *Wisdom and knowledge will be the stability*
> *of your times,*
> *and the strength of salvation;*
> *the fear of the Lord is His treasure*
> *(see Isaiah 33:6; also see 11:2).*
> *If any of you lacks wisdom,*
> *Let him ask of God,*

Who gives to all liberally and
Without reproach,
And it will be given to him (see James 1:3).

The wisdom of God gives us not necessarily information on how to get out of trouble but rather revelation on how to learn from one's difficulties. Satan is in the world. Listen to the apostle John, *"You are of God, little children, and have overcome them: because greater is he that is in you, than he that is in the world" (1 John 4:4).* Wisdom listens to Jesus, *"Abide in Me, and I in you. As the branch cannot bear fruit of itself, unless it abides in the vine, neither can you, unless you abide in Me" (John 15:4).* We are to reject any independence from God even in thought. In fact it is wise to nurture an increasingly deeper relationship with Jesus Christ.

In Proverbs 29:15, the words "rod" and "rebuke" both speak of correction or discipline. An undisciplined child shames everyone, especially his or her parents. Verse 17 places the burden of correction on the parents. Delight here speaks of rich, delicious food (see Genesis 49:20).

Satan and his demons are overwhelming many Christians and churches today under the weight of growing frustrations, discouragements, and increasing compromise. The real problem is not sin that caused the defeat, but biblical ignorance. Jesus gave demonstrations of His lessons to be learned by His disciples before He sent them out:

- They saw Him cast out demons. He sent them to do the same.
- Before sending them out, He charged them to become wise as serpents and harmless as doves (see Matthew 10:16).
- This fusion of divine wisdom and Christ-like innocence is the taproot of all spiritual victory.

We must learn the ways of God, which means we must think with wisdom. This requires that we be pure in heart, so that we may see God and gain discernment. Remember, it is *ignorance* of God's truth that leaves us vulnerable to satanic attack. Wisdom gives us some valued advice:

- Whatever high and lofty spiritual levels you think you are on remember Adam and Eve were in the Garden of Eden when they fell.

- Before your increased knowledge and religious experiences make you overly self-confident remember Solomon wrote three books of Scripture, yet he fell.
- Yes, even in your deepest worship of almighty God, don't forget in long ages past Lucifer himself was once in heaven pouring out praises to God. He fell!

It is wisdom to recognize that we don't know all there is to know concerning warfare. Listen to the Holy Spirit speaking, *"There was a small city with a few men in it and a great king came to it, surrounded it, and constructed large siege-works against it. But there was found in it a poor wise man and he delivered the city by wisdom (see Ecclesiastes 9:14-15). Wisdom is better than strength . . . wisdom is better than weapons of war (vv. 18, 19).*

Basic Requirements before Battle

Just before Jesus went to His death, He remarked, *"the ruler of this world is coming, and he has nothing in Me" (John 14:30).* Satan has nothing in Jesus Christ. We also want to be able to say that Satan has nothing in us. He tries to implant *"exciter buttons"* in the minds of Christians so that he can push them and open the door of our soul to sin. We have discussed the relationship between the spirit and the soul once we are born again. This spiritual conflict necessitates our understanding of that fact for victory. We will walk in great victory if we are obedient to this passage, *"Walk in the Spirit and you shall not fulfill the lust of the flesh" (see Galatians 5:16-17).*

The Scriptures make it clear, either we are walking in the Spirit or we are walking in the flesh. The unregenerate person can only walk in the flesh because he or she is not born again. However, the born again Christian can walk in the flesh and he or she can walk in the Spirit. This unstableness is dangerous ground on which to walk. In Galatians 5:17-23 Paul contrasts characteristics of these two walks:

Walking in the flesh (Satan's domain) vv. 19-21 lists seventeen works of the flesh:

- Adultery—unlawful sexual relations (Galatians 5:19; Matthew 5:32; 15:19).
- Fornication—all manner of other unlawful relations (Matthew 5:32).
- Uncleanness—all forms of sexual perversion (v. 16; Romans 1:21-32; 6:19).
- Lasciviousness—anything tending to promote sex sin (v. 19; 2 Peter 2:7).
- Idolatry—passionate affections upon things (Galatians 5:20; Col. 3:5).
- Witchcraft—practice of dealing with evil spirits (v. 20; Revelation 22:15).
- Hatred—bitter dislike; abhorrence (v. 20; Ephesians 2:15-16).
- Variance—discord, dissensions, quarreling (v. 20; Romans 1:29).
- Emulations—envies, jealousies, outdo others, zeal (v. 20; Romans 10:2).
- Wrath—indignation, fierceness (v. 20; Ephesians 4:31, Col. 3:8).
- Strife—contentions, pay back (v. 20; 1 Corinthians 12:20).
- Seditions—disorder, parties, divisions (v. 20; 1 Corinthians 3:3).
- Heresies—goes astray from truth (v. 20; Acts 5:17; Galatians 2).
- Envying—jealous of others blessings (v. 21: Matthew 27:18).
- Murders—to kill; hatred (v. 21; 1 John 3:15).
- Drunkenness—living intoxicated (v. 21; Romans 13:13).
- Reveling—rioting, sinful activities (v.21; 1 Peter 4:3; Romans 13:13).

When the above destructive behavior is portrayed in the Christian, it is positive proof that he or she is not walking in the power of the Spirit (vv. 16, 18, 23) but is being energized by Satan or his demons (see Matthew 16:23; Acts 5:3). We must remember that spiritual warfare rages between our two ears, in our minds. Pray for wisdom. This person's mind has not been fully transformed! Paul goes on to say, *"those who practice such things will not inherit the kingdom of God (v. 21).* That's the Word! Unless this individual confesses and put these sins out of their life; they will not inherit the kingdom (see 1 Corinthians 6:9-11).

Philosophers and academia has redefined the word tolerance to coincide with society's moral conclusion that the absolutes for which it should strive has decreed that everything is legitimate as long as it doesn't hinder or harm others. This is the fruit of their enlightenment that there is no real right and wrong; therefore, the thinking is that we must tolerate everything. Therefore we find the works of the flesh being accepted as normal behavior even in some of the local assemblies under the disguise of progressive thinking. As citizens of the kingdom of God, we can expect conflict with the domain of Satan. Truth by its very nature is intolerant! Those of us who are committed to truth will always tolerate those persons who are in error but will never tolerate the error itself. In spite of societal demands, if we are to be like Christ, our King, to the glory of God in this world; then we must leave the penetrating impression that He left on earth. He was full of truth (see John 1:14) and His truth was the reflected glory of His Father. The Source of the truth that we stand in is the Holy Spirit and the authoritative Word. We are at war!

The Scriptures distinctly state that the only way to overcome these fleshy desires is to live in the power of the Holy Spirit as He works through our spirit (see Galatians 5:25). Walking each moment by faith in God's Word under the Holy Spirit's control; you *shall not* fulfill the lusts of the flesh (see Galatians 5:16). God has provided a way out; so don't be deceived; there is no excuse for compromise or hypocrisy (see Galatians 6:7-8). Walking in the Spirit (Christ's domain) vv. 22-23 lists the nine-fold fruit of the Spirit:

- Love—esteem, devotion, mutuality (v.22; 1 Corinthians 13; Romans 8:28).
- Joy—rejoice even among the worse circumstances (v. 22; Philippians 4:11).
- Peace—keep hearts and minds, no anxiety (v. 22; Philippians 4:7).
- Longsuffering—power under control (v. 22; II Corinthians 6:3-10).
- Kindness—goodness, patience (v. 22; 1 Corinthians 13:4).
- Goodness—righteousness (v. 22; Romans 15:14; II Thessalonians 1:11).
- Faithfulness—faithful, faith Galatians 5:22; 3:10).
- Gentleness—meekness, submissive, teachable (v. 22; II Corinthians 10:1).
- Self-control—temperance, self-mastery (1 Corinthians 7:9; 10:23, 31).

In introducing the above list of character traits of the Christian, Paul uses the singular *fruit*, whereas in speaking of the flesh, *works* are plural. The sinful nature is rebellious against God and mixed in purposes splitting life into fragments. In regeneration the Holy Spirit integrates your life with God and people, centering in the *unifying* love of Christ. Thus each of the nine-fold fruit of the Spirit is simply love in another form, a revelation of the character of God through Christ and through Christians. Paul warned that without the fruit no person could enter the kingdom of heaven. Without these godly character qualities the Christian does not glorify God in this world. Christ is our only Example!

God went through great lengths to get Christians to walk in the Spirit; yet many are carnally-minded finding themselves being conformed or shaped by a secular worldview. Why? Because they do not diligently seek the revelation of God's Word (see II Peter 1:1-3; 1 Peter 1:18-21). The Scriptures warn that God's people perish from a lack of [biblical] knowledge. These Christians use the same references for their understanding as the world, sight through (Science and reason) in their attempt to access that knowledge received only by revelation. That is disastrous, because Christ is not their Source. Earlier the apostle Paul called these Christians walking by sight carnal. Carnality means they live closer to the world in their thinking than to the truth of God's Word, simply because they fail to study and obey the Bible for mind renewing spiritual growth.

Free from indwelling sin

Earlier I pointed out that Paul made it clear the major problem causing the individual to be tossed to and fro is the *flesh* guided by the *soulish* five senses (see, hear, smell, taste, and feel). He is jubilant because there is victory through Christ Jesus, who delivers us from this body of death (the flesh), also called the old man. From this argument Paul moves into the solution namely, salvation found only in Jesus Christ (see Romans 7:25).

In contrast He points out the freedom of living in the Spirit. There is no condemnation because we are empowered by the Spirit to live for Christ (see Romans 8:1). Let's notice a profile of the Christian who is free from indwelling sin:

- This Christian is "born again" otherwise seeing and understanding the kingdom of God is impossible (see John 3:3).
- This Christian is not conformed or shaped by worldly thinking (the flesh), would cause the individual to see the Word of God through the circumstances of life; but rather he or she through a renewed mind sees their circumstances through the Word of God, the Bible (see Romans 12:1, 2).
- This Christian is a new creation, all things are become new including a new divine human nature (see 2 Corinthians 5:17).
- This Christian has put on the new man who is renewed in knowledge according to the image of Him who created him or her (see Colossians 3:10).
- This Christian is complete in Christ in whom the fullness of the Godhead dwells bodily (see Colossians 2:9-10).
- This Christian's needs come through the knowledge of God (see 1 Peter 1:3-4).
- This Christian has the Spirit of Christ in his or her heart (see Galatians 4:6).
- This Christian who is joined to the Lord is one spirit with Him (see 1 Corinthians 6:17).
- This Christian has an anointing from the Holy One and knows all things (see 1 John 2:20), and he or she has the power of Christ (see Ephesians 1:18-19).
- This Christian has the mind of Christ (see 1 Corinthians 2:16).

How is this possible? Through our blood-washed spirit, and renewed soul and body that is now complete in Christ!

Fit to Fight

The Holy Spirit has empowered and equipped God's people for service (see Acts 1:8). Jesus promised the Spirit would be given to His followers following His resurrection. This was manifested when the Holy Spirit came upon all who believed (see Acts 2). The power of God within enables us to do spiritual battle. I want to point out that spiritual warfare waged today is victorious only on the basis of appropriating the provision of the Cross and Christ's blood (see Colossians 2:15).

Ephesians 6 gives us a look into the very nature of the spiritual warfare we face daily. Our combat is against spiritual foes, not mere humans. However, God has provided great protection and all the resources in our born again spirit needed to successfully face this enemy. Paul admonishes, put on the whole armor of God, that you may be able to "stand against" meaning to aggressively hold at bay or to stand in front of and oppose or fit to fight in one on one combat.

Using a metaphor based on the Roman soldier with whom he was well acquainted; since he was guarded by one for two years. Paul had ample time to study the function of each piece of the soldier's armor. There is a very important observation that I can pass on about these pieces of body armor; having spent 26.5 years in the U.S. Army. Body armor used by today's combat soldiers though technologically advanced has the same basic functions as that used by the Roman soldiers Paul observed 2000 years ago.

How much more enduring then is the armor of God! You are to use every piece of God's armor to resist the enemy in the time of evil, so that when the battle is over you will be standing firm awaiting the next encounter. All of this armor is not just a passive protection in facing the enemy; it is to be used offensively against satanic forces. Remember, the battle is in your mind!

- The first piece of armor is the belt of *truth,* for it is truth that refutes Satan's lies and exposes his deceptions. Always remember Satan is the father of lies (John 8:44). One of his favorite tactics is to question God's word. "Did God really say . . . ?" So to counter his lies it is imperative that we know the truth. We must earnestly study and obey God's word to show ourselves approved unto God. Then we are able to speak the truth in love and confess our sins when we have failed (see 1 John 1:9). We acknowledge the fact, that only truth you know will set you free (John 8:32). The soldier has life sustaining items attached to the belt all pointing to *truth:* the Sword representative of the cutting ability of God's truth; the canteen of water representative of the life sustaining ability of truth; the first aid packet representative of the power and healing ability of the God's truth for those wounded physically and spiritually. We leave no room for the deceiver in our hearts, we take God's

Word as true and trustworthy and that settles it! Remember God has objectively defeated Satan and his demonic agenda!

- The second piece of armor is to "put on God's *righteousness.*" *He made Him who knew no sin to be sin for us, that we might become the righteousness of God in Him (2 Corinthians 5:21).* Here, we are in fact made righteous, forgiven, and accepted in the beloved through faith in Jesus Christ alone. Our confidence is in what God has already done for us in Jesus Christ through His death and resurrection. The next time you have the opportunity to see a group of soldiers in formation, the first thing that should strike you is the fact they are all in the same uniform. Righteousness is the uniform of the saints. As we grow in faith, we learn to flee temptation and exercise self-control. We break free from the penalty and power of sin (see Romans 6:11-16). James says, *"Lay aside all filthiness and overflow of wickedness, and receive with meekness the implanted word, which is able to save your souls" (James 1:21).* While we continually respond to the sanctifying truth that God shows us about His transforming will for our lives; we are to live a righteous life, knowing that our hope is our faith in Jesus Christ.

- The third piece of armor is to have our feet shod with the preparation of the *gospel of peace.* Isaiah 52:7 says, "How beautiful on the mountains are the feet of those who bring the good news of peace and salvation, the news that the God of Israel reigns!" As we enter spiritual battle, our walk depends upon boots cushioned from the shock of rocks or any other ground obstacles that would slow our progress. When you align your soul under the rule of your spirit which is God's order, God will release His peace into your life because the peace of Christ is now ruling your thoughts and conduct. Remember we will never experience Christ's victory in its fullness until we stop reacting humanly to our circumstances. The gospel of peace should always mediate between the world and us. No matter the terrain smooth, rocky, flat, or hilly, we walk in the power of the gospel, which illumines our path, and carries us to our objective; which is to clearly understand and readily advance the kingdom of God by sharing the gospel message of peace. Peace is Spirit power!

- The fourth piece of armor is the *shield of faith* which provides a covering for the entire body of the soldier. The next time you see the police or soldiers during riot control you will notice that they carry a large shield to protect their bodies from rocks, Molotov cocktails, or any other objects hurled at them. The faith Paul speaks of in this context means absolute confidence in God, his promises, his power, and his plan for our lives. Believers must continually trust in God's word and promises to protect them from temptations to every kind of sin. All sin comes from falling for Satan's lies and rejecting the better choice of obedience and blessings. Note some of the fiery darts Satan will throw at you; and remember the battle is in your mind:

- Hateful thoughts
- Unresolved anger
- Doubts about God and the Bible
- Doubts about Jesus as the only way
- Doubts about provision
- Overwhelming times of depression
- Inferior among others
- Embedded false beliefs from significant others

Sometimes it's necessary to link shields together building a wall. We are encouraged to come together agreeing in prayers of intercession about someone or something, it surely blocks Satan. We also take cover behind the shield of faith to protect us against temptation, accusations, and persecutions the evil one fires off at us. Faith destroys the darts of doubt and deception. By faith we have the mind of Christ (see 1 Corinthians 2:16). By faith we trust the Lord's protection and victory over sin and demonic activity. Claiming God's promises by faith, trusting in His unchanging character, and holding up His truth will deflect and extinguish the enemy's lies. Psalm 91 is one of the Christian soldier's best expressions of faith in battle. We accelerate our faith with the truth of God's Word. Think of the dart that has pierced your life in the past. Which of God's promises could have saved you from the wound you received?

- The fifth piece of armor is the *helmet of salvation.* In salvation there are two definitions. The first has to do with Jesus Christ healing us from the mortal wound of sin. The second meaning denotes our deliverance from the captivity of the enemy. All armies equip their soldiers with helmets and the reason is obvious. The helmet of salvation protects our minds and thoughts. In Romans 12:2, Paul instructs us not to be conformed to this world but to be transformed by the renewing of our minds. Don't let the world mold your worldview. God will do it in us if we let him. The helmet of salvation is the certainty of deliverance from sin and protection of our minds in battle. We have three phases of salvation in the New Testament:

- We have been saved (see Justification in Romans 8:24; Ephesians 2:8).
- We are being saved (see Sanctification in 1 Corinthians 1:18)
- We will be saved (see Glorification in 1 Corinthians 3:15; 1 Peter 1:5).

Paul also refers to the helmet of salvation as an expression of hope (see 1Thessalonians 5:8-9).

- The sixth piece of armor is the *sword of the Spirit;* we can cut the devil's defenses with the sword of the Spirit, the Word of God. Most places in the New Testament Greek; "word" is translated "logos." Here in Ephesians 6:17, it is translated "rhema." God applies his Word (rhema) by making the Word (logos) alive and active in our specific situations. We can see this sword or (rhema) in action in Jesus' response to Satan's temptations in the wilderness. In response to every temptation, Jesus replied, "It is written," (see Matthew 4:4, 6, 10). The Word (rhema) cuts through the lies Satan attempts to cast our way. That is what "resist the devil" means. You counter lies with truth, and truth always wins! Of the six pieces of armor listed the sword is our only *offensive* weapon (see Hebrews 4:12-13). The psalmist said, "How can a young man keep his way pure? By keeping it according to your Word . . . Thy Word have I hid in my heart, that I might not sin against You" (Psalm 119:11). Meditate on God's word day and night (see Joshua 1:8).

Paul ends this discourse with a call to prayer. Take up the whole armor of God in order to maintain a "battle ready stance" against satanic forces. Give yourself to constant, faithful, fervent prayer. Let God change your prayer life to a life of prayer. Prayer is to include supplication in the Spirit (see Romans 8:26, 27). Prayer is not a part of the armor it is the *battle* through which we are continually armed, supplied, directed, and restored. Engaging in the battle itself is the purpose for which we are armed. Paul admonishes us to stay alert and be persistent in your prayers for all Christians everywhere (see Ephesians 6:18). Again, prayer is the battle itself; and God's Word is our chief offensive weapon employed against Satan during our struggle. Without prayer, all the armor in the world would be of no use. Pray always!

Personal Journal Notes
(Reflection & Response)

1. The most important thing I learned from this chapter was:

2. The area that I need to work on the most is:

3. I can apply this lesson to my life by:

4. Closing statement of Commitment:

CHAPTER FOURTEEN

Resurrections and Judgments

The revelation of God in Scripture shows that God is eternal, and not limited by time. Moses said, *"From everlasting to everlasting thou art God . . . For a thousand years in thy sight are but as yesterday when it is past, and as a watch in the night"* (see Psalm 90:2, 4) KJV. God said of Himself, *"I AM THAT I AM"* (see Exodus 3:14-15). He is the first and the last, the beginning and the ending, the Alpha and the Omega (see Revelation 1:8; Isaiah 41:4). Unlike God, humanity is subject to time; therefore finite and limited by time and space. Humanity had a beginning but exists eternally. Every individual will be rewarded by God according to his or her works during their span of life whether they are good or bad.

The Probation of Humans (Time)

Between the birth and death of every child of Adam, there is a span of life. It is during this period of time, known *only* to God that each individual is on probation. As we saw earlier God placed Adam and Eve on probation in the Garden of Eden with one commandment, they failed (see Genesis 2:17; 3:1-6). God pronounced the death penalty on their sin of disobedience. He extended *grace* to them and gave them space to repent and be restored to His fellowship by the sacrificial blood of a Substitute. It is this *"the space to repent"* which is given to every one born of Adam (see Revelation 2:21). No man knows how long this *"space"* is and it is the grace of God which comes to every individual during this time seeking to lead him or her to repentance (see II Peter 3:8-9).

The apostle Paul alludes to this time as a dispensation meaning "administration of a household or stewardship" given by God (see I Corinthians 9:1-7; Ephesians 1:10; 3:2; Colossians 1:25). God has a plan of stewardship for each of us who are called according to His purpose in time (see Romans 8:28). Once this period of time is over the person dies and his or her probation is over forever. Thus, their eternal state and destiny are settled and unchangeable. God exemplified in time what He will do in eternity. God issues certain judgments and rewards in *time* to both the righteous and the unrighteous. He follows the same principle in eternity.

Two Resurrections and the Judgments

The resurrections and the judgments of God are entwined. They cannot be separated. Resurrection precedes judgment and judgment makes resurrection necessary. Thus this truth involves "the resurrection of the dead and eternal judgment" (see Hebrews 6:1-2; Revelation 20:1-15). There are two resurrections spoken of in the New and Old Testaments coming to the whole human race:

1.   **Resurrection of the Righteous**
     • The First Resurrection Revelation 20:4-6).
     • The Resurrection of the Just (Acts 24:15; Luke 14:14).
     • The Resurrection of Life (John 5:29).
     • The Awakening to Everlasting Life (Daniel 12:2).
     • The Better Resurrection (Hebrews 11:35).
2.   **Resurrection of the Unrighteous**
     • The Second Resurrection (Revelation 20:4-6).
     • Resurrection of the Unjust (Acts 24:15).
     • The Resurrection of Damnation (John 5:29).
     • The Awakening to shame and Everlasting Contempt (Daniel 12:2).

The apostle John informs us that these two resurrections are a thousand years apart. He said, *"Blessed* and *holy* are they who have part in the first resurrection."* They are judged and receive eternal life and rewards according to their character and works in Christ. The people of the second resurrection are *cursed* and *unholy*. They are judged and sentenced to eternal damnation according to their character and works in this life. The justice, righteousness and holiness of God's law demand that He judge sin. This He does in three aspects:

1. **Judgment Past**
    *   At Calvary, judgment was legally and judicially executed upon Satan and his demonic hosts (see Colossians 2:14-15; John 12:31; 14:30; 16:11).
    *   At Calvary, the sins of the world were judged by Christ's death and all who believe in Jesus know that they have passed from death to life. Christ was judged for them (see John 5:24; II Corinthians 5:21; Galatians 3:13; 1 Peter 2:24).

2. **Judgment Present**
    *   There is a present judgment going on in the earth. In relation to the ungodly, God often steps in and judges the sins of men. Though sin contains its own judgment, the final judgment is yet to come.
    *   The believers are to judge themselves so that they will not come into judgment with the world.
    *   God also divinely disciplines and chastens His people (see 1 Corinthians 11:31-32; 5:5; 1 Timothy 1:20; Hebrews 12:1-10).

3. **Judgment Future**
    *   Many Scriptures speak of a future judgment. All nations and cultures have this built into their understanding and conscience. All will be judged in absolute justice (see 1 Corinthians 3:8-16; 4:5; II Corinthians 5:10; Hebrews 10:27; Acts 24:25).

The Day of Judgment, the great reckoning day when God will bring all men before His throne to give an account of their lives as lived here on earth (see Acts 17:31; Romans 2:16; II Peter 3:7; Psalm 96:13). Thus all human beings good or bad will be judged. They will be eternally separated into two groups. These groups are "the sheep" and "the goats" (Matthew 25:33) "the just" and the "wicked" (Matthew 13:49); "the saints" and "those who obey not the Gospel" (II Thessalonians 1:8-10). All will be eternally "blessed" or "cursed" (Matthew 25:34, 41). The two destinies will be *either* heaven or hell!

Personal Journal Notes
(Reflection & Response)

1. The most important thing I learned from this chapter is:

2. The area that I need to work on the most is:

3. I can apply this lesson to my life by:

4. Closing statement of Commitment:

CHAPTER FIFTEEN

Rewards and Judgments

The Word of God states that all believers and unbelievers are to be judged and rewarded by the omniscient Jesus Christ. He has all the hidden facts, deeds, motives and thoughts of men, women, boys and girls before Him. As stated in the last chapter, the two judgments and reward ceremonies of the believers and unbelievers will be separated by a thousand years.

The Judgment and Rewards of Believers

Concerning the judgments and rewards of the saints, God has made many promises of reward to His people. Please understand it is not that the believer works for the reward. There is a saying throughout the church, "We do not work to be saved, but we work because we are saved!" We must get rid of that deception of human works in our salvation (see Ephesians 2:8-9). Neither should there be any thought of wrong motives, nor thinking that God uses the promise of rewards as a bribe. The rewards are promises out of God's love and they are held up as rewards for a race well run, or a work well done:

1. Judgment of the Believers
All believers must appear before the *Judgment Seat of Christ* and give an account of themselves and their works (see I Corinthians 3:11-15; II Corinthians 5:10-11).

- The Lord desires that we be bold in our day of judgment and not ashamed before Him at His coming (1 John 4:17; II Timothy 4:1, 8: Revelation 11:18).

FIGURE #1

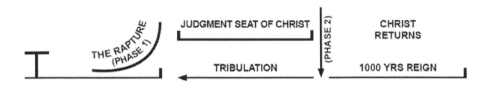

This judgment actually takes place after the *phase 1 of His Second Coming:* Notice in Figure 1 above, Christ will come in the air and *His Church will be "caught up" (Rapture)* to meet Him in the air (see 1 Thessalonians 4:15-18; Matthew 24:30-31).

After the *Rapture of the Church* there will be a seven year (tribulation) period in which God will complete Israel's history (see Revelation 6-18; Matthew 24:21). At the end of the seven years *Christ returns in His phase 2*; this time He will come to the earth, His saints with Him to rule the world for a thousand years (see Revelation 20:2-3).

- Please know that this judgment does not concern the believer's salvation, for *that was settled* at Calvary; it is a judgment of his or her works and service for the Lord (see Revelation 19:6-10). The apostle Paul frequently used the Grecian Olympic Games to illustrate his message. After the games were over, the winners were assembled before the "Judgment Seat" of the Judge to receive the victor's crown. Not all of the contestants received a victor's crown.

2. Rewards of the Believers

Listed below are the rewards for the believer, which are given according to their faithfulness and service to the Lord during their life span on earth (see Ephesians 6:2):

- The reward of faithfulness (Matthew 25:21-23).

- The reward of the crown of life (James 1:12; Revelation 2:10).
- The reward of the crown of glory (I Peter 5:2-4; Hebrews 2:9).
- The reward of the crown of rejoicing (I Thessalonians 2:19-20).
- The reward of the crown of righteousness (II Timothy 4:8).
- The reward of the incorruptible crown (I Corinthians 9:25-27; I John 2:28).
- The reward of the prophet and the righteous man (Matthew 10:41-42).
- The reward of God's saints and servants (Revelation 11:18).
- The Crowns of gold (Revelation 4:4; 3:11).

"They overcame him by the blood of the Lamb and by the word of their testimony" (Revelation 12:11). No accusation can stand against those whose sins have been forgiven because of the blood of the Lamb (see Romans 8:33-39).

The Judgment and Rewards of the Unbelievers

That the unbelievers are to come up for judgment is necessary by the very nature of the human race. Many things have escaped judgment during the unbeliever's life time. If God did not bring them to judgment it would be a violation of His justice, righteousness, and holy law. The *character* and *deeds* of the ungodly, which so often escaped judgment in time, demands that God bring every work into judgment, and He will at the Great White Throne Judgment (see Revelation 20:11-15).

1. The Judgment of Unbelievers
The judgment of the ungodly will take place at **the Great White Throne** (**Figure 2 below**) at the close of the 1000 year kingdom reign of Christ on the earth (Revelation 20:11-15).

FIGURE #2

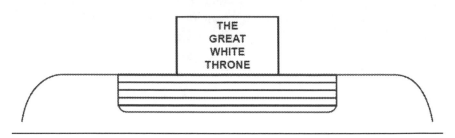

All are judged out of the books according to their works (Daniel 7:10, 22-26; Acts 24:28; Jude 14-15).

2. The Rewards of the Unbelievers

The Lord said He would reward the wicked according to their works. Review the Scriptures concerning the following two examples: Balaam received the "reward and wages of unrighteousness" (II Peter 2:13-15). Judas received the "reward of iniquity" (Acts 1:18). So, all the godless and wicked will receive their "reward" according to their evil deeds.

Personal Journal Notes (Reflection & Response)

1. The most important thing I learned from this chapter is:

2. The area that I need to work on the most is:

3. I can apply this lesson to my life by:

4. Closing statement of Commitment:

CHAPTER SIXTEEN

Eternal Dwelling Places

The punishment of the wicked and the rewarding of the righteous are seen in the places which Scripture call heaven and hell. Heaven is the eternal dwelling place of the righteous; while Hell is the eternal dwelling place of the wicked. These are the ultimate rewards. Many people want to believe in a heaven without a hell, but it is inconsistent to have one without the other.

The Dwelling Place of the Unredeemed (Hell)

Hell is the place of final punishment of the wicked; of all who die in their sins and unregenerate condition (see Revelation 20:12-15).

- Hell is actually a place, as surely as heaven is a place (see Matthew 5:22, 29-30; 10:28; 18:9; 23:15). Many like to accept heaven while rejecting hell as a place. God has a place of happiness for the redeemed who serve Him. Likewise God has a place of punishment for the rebellious who serve the devil. Jesus spoke more about hell than all other Bible writers, and why not? He came to save humanity from it!
- Hell was not made for humankind but actually for the devil and his angels. If people choose to serve the devil in this life, then they will dwell eternally with him in hell (see Matthew 25:41).

- Sheol or Hades is "the place of departed human spirits" (unsaved souls) since the resurrection of Christ, as well as Old Testament unregenerate persons. All are awaiting final judgment at the Great White Throne and sentencing eternally to *"The Lake of Fire" Figure 3 below* (see Revelation 19:20; 20:10, 14, 15; 21:8).

FIGURE 3

SATAN   ANTICHRIST   FALSE PROPHET

UNHOLY ANGELS   ALL UNBELIEVERS

FIRE & BRIMSTONE   ETERNAL TORMENT

ETERNAL CONSCIOUSNESS OF SINS

ETERNAL SEPARATION FROM GOD

The New Testament speaks of what this eternal home of the unregenerate will be like:

- Hell will be the valley of the dead bodies and souls of the unregenerate (see Matthew 5:29-30; 18:9; Luke 12:5).
- Hell will be the valley of groans, weeping and wailing of the lost of the human race (see Matthew 13:42, 50).
- Hell will be a place for hypocrites, serpents in character (see Matthew 23:14, 15, 33). • Hell will be a place of fire and brimstone (Revelation 19:20; 20:10, 14-15; 21:8).
- Hell will be a place of horrible torment (see Revelation 14:9-11; Luke 16:19).
- Hell will be a place of continually ascending smoke (see Revelation 14:10-11).
- Hell will be a fire that is never quenched (see Mark 9:43-49).

- Hell is a place where "the worm" of conscience never dies (see Isaiah 66:24; Psalm 21:9; Job 24:20 with Acts 12:20-23; Mark 9:43-48).
- Hell was prepared for the devil and his angels. Therefore the unredeemed will find it a place of vile company (see Isaiah 30:33; II Peter 2:4; Jude 6; Matthew 25:41, 46; Revelation 21:8).
- Hell is for all those whose names are not found written in the Book of Life (see Revelation 2:11; 20:14; 21:8; 20:11-15).
- Hell is called the second death (see Revelation 2:11; 20:11-15; 21:8).
- Hell will be a place of everlasting shame and contempt (see Daniel 12:2; Romans 2:16).
- Hell will be a furnace of fire (see Matthew 13:42, 50; 25:41, 46).

Hell will be a terrible place separate from the presence of God, the rejected Lamb, the holy angels and the redeemed. No light, life, peace, joy, righteousness, nor salvation, but only darkness and torment will be there for those who have rejected and despised the blood of the Lamb, the grace of God.

- This is the hell that Jesus died to save us from!
- Hell is a self-chosen and self-inflicted curse, the inevitable outcome of sin.

The Dwelling Place of the Redeemed (Heaven)

Heaven is the dwelling place of God and the elect angels. It is also the everlasting home of the redeemed of all humanity. Here the believer is promised:

- The Tree of life (Revelation 2:7).
- Not to be hurt of the second death (Revelation 2:11).
- A stone with a new name in it (Revelation 2:17).
- Authority with Christ (Revelation 2:26-27).
- A white garment and his or her name in the Book of Life (Revelation 3:12).
- Security in the City of God (Revelation 3:12).

- And ruling and reigning in the Throne of God and the Lamb (Revelation 3:21)

Wherever Jesus is that is heaven. See Figure 4 below. Heaven will be a place of:

FIGURE 4

THE FATHER THE SON THE HOLY SPIRIT
THE HOLY ANGELS

"the redeemed from all the ages of time"

"light"   "love"   "holiness"

"righteousness"   "worship"   "service"

"joy"   "praise"   "peace"   "life"

"no sin" "no sorrows"

"eternity"

Jesus said He was going *"to prepare a place for you, I will come again and receive you to Myself; that where I am, there you may be also" (John 14:3)*. Think of it, spending eternity with our Redeemer! What a wonderful and worthy reward. Come LORD JESUS!

Personal Journal Notes (Reflection & Response)

1. The most important thing I learned from this chapter was:

2. The area that I need to work on the most is:

3. I can apply this lesson to my life by:

4. Closing statement of Commitment